A Glossary of Phonology

A Glossary of Phonology

Philip Carr

Edinburgh University Press

Edinburgh University Press Ltd
22 George Square, Edinburgh

Typeset in Sabon
by Servis Filmsetting Ltd, Stockport, Cheshire, and
printed and bound in Great Britain by
CPI Antony Rowe, Chippenham

A CIP record for this book is available from the British Library

ISBN 978 0 7486 2404 1 (hardback)
ISBN 978 0 7486 2234 4 (paperback)

Published with the support of the Edinburgh University Scholarly
Publishing Initiatives Fund.

Contents

Introduction

When I agreed to write this little book, I imagined that it would be easier to put together than a textbook. I was wrong. In a textbook, one can tell the reader the following sort of thing: 'Recall our discussion of this phenomenon in chapter 2; now we'll look at it in more detail.' That cannot be done in a glossary, since it has no narrative structure. And while elementary textbooks require a good deal of simplification, a glossary is bound to be even more simplified, since the entries have to be kept relatively short. None the less, I hope that the definitions given here are accurate, if simplified, and will be of some help to students engaging with a discipline which can appear to have a dauntingly large amount of specialised terminology.

I have chosen to focus on what I take to be phonological phenomena: that is, the kinds of states of affairs which phonologists believe they have often observed in human languages, such as, say vowel nasalisation. In doing so, I have adopted the process metaphor; many of the phenomena in question are described as processes. Because I wish to focus on what I take to be phenomena, I have tried to avoid defining phonological notions in terms of properties of diagrams. Phonologists are fond of diagrams for understandable reasons; human beings find it helpful to be able to depict, and thus visualise, abstract notions. But I believe that one should not mistake the diagrams for the phenomena under investigation. Since the focus is on phonological phenomena, I have not attempted to list every theoretical construct postulated in the history of phonology. When one considers the vast number of such constructs, particularly in the field of generative phonology, the task would anyway have been impossible, given the space limitations.

It is with the most fundamental, elementary terms in linguistics that the most difficult issues arise. An example is the definition of the word 'phonology' itself. The fact is that there is controversy as to exactly what we take the discipline and its object of inquiry to be. I have not sought to sweep such controversy under the carpet. Rather, I have tried to explain, in relatively simple terms, what the different, often competing, conceptions are. One of the issues here is the question of whether a valid distinction can be drawn between phonetics and phonology. And if such a distinction can be drawn, how is it to be drawn, and what might the relation be between these two areas? These are difficult, controversial issues, and I have not hesitated to convey that fact to the reader. Since I believe that we do need to distinguish phonetics and phonology, and assuming that a glossary of phonetics will be forthcoming in this glossary series, I have not attempted a systematic coverage of phonetic terminology. Rather, I have given definitions for phonetic terms as and when I needed to use them.

Related to the kinds of controversy which exist in the field of phonology is the status of expressions such as 'mentalism' and other 'isms'. The moment one tries to define expressions such as 'phonology' or 'phoneme', one has to explain that there are mentalistic and non-mentalistic conceptions of these, and different kinds of mentalistic conception. I have therefore included brief definitions of various 'isms' in order to help the reader understand what lies behind the various different conceptions of notions such as 'phoneme'. One would not, of course, think of turning to a glossary of phonology if one were seeking a brief definition of, say, Empiricism. But the Empiricist vs Rationalist debate has formed part of the background to the development of phonological theory and theories as to how children acquire a phonological system, so I have given an indication of what that debate is about. I have also done this because I do not believe that phonology should be taught in an intellectual vacuum, cut off from other disciplines. The history of the discipline also constitutes part of the intellectual context in which phonology should be studied. I have therefore included brief definitions of various schools of thought which have existed in the history of phonology, such as the Prague School, founded in the mid-1920s. In connection with this, I have given brief sketches of prominent phonologists, from the nineteenth century to the present day. There was no way of knowing just how many such figures to cite, or of knowing the extent to which a given phonologist could be described as 'prominent'. I do hope, however, that the reader will have been given at least some idea of who has been associated with which ideas. The discipline is as much about people and places as it is about ideas. My apologies to phonologists who believe that they are major figures in the field, but whose names do not appear here.

In choosing words, phrases and sentences for the purposes of exemplification, I have tried to stick with languages which I purport to know something about, mostly English and French. But there are many phonological phenomena which are simply not attested in either of those languages, and for those phenomena, I have had to resort to primary and secondary sources, which are cited at the end of the book. There is a great danger in citing examples from languages one is not familiar with, but there is no way around it if one is to achieve a decent coverage of the kinds of phonological phenomena found in the world's languages. The result of my attempting to exemplify notions from English and French is that there is a bias towards English in this glossary. This should not be interpreted as an attempt to convey the idea that English is somehow superior to, more important than, or more worthy of study than other languages.

It will be evident to teachers that this book has been written by someone with a background in British descriptive traditions. However, I have not, I hope, fallen into a kind of British insularity; there is a good deal of coverage of notions used in European and North American descriptive traditions. Where there are differences between British and American descriptive traditions, I have attempted to indicate what those are.

Since I believe that the discipline of phonology overlaps with other disciplines, I have given brief accounts, where I deemed it necessary and/or useful, of some notions from the fields of child language acquisition, historical linguistics, morphology, sociolinguistics and syntax. I have also tried to ensure that there is a degree of consistency between the definitions of morphological, sociolinguistic and syntactic terms given here and those given in Laurie Bauer's *A Glossary of Morphology*, Geoffrey Leech's *A Glossary of English Grammar* and Peter Trudgill's *A Glossary of Sociolinguistics*.

I have included informal terms such as 'smoothing' (monophthongisation) when they are relatively widely used and can be given a clear definition. Informal terms used in ordinary everyday speech have been included if they are meaningful and are also used by linguists. The term 'broad', used to refer to certain accents, has therefore been included. Other informal terms used by the lay person have been omitted because they cannot be given a clear definition. Examples are terms such as 'twang', 'drawl' and 'flattened vowels'. Such terms are, in my view, used to refer to such a disparate range of phonetic/phonological properties as to be more or less meaningless.

Cross-referenced terms are in **bold**. Words, phrases and sentences given as examples are in *italics*. Glosses (English translations of non-English words) are given in inverted commas. Where a general phenomenon, such as intervocalic voicing or nasalisation, is discussed, the entry is given in lower case. Where I am describing a process which has been postulated for a specific language, such as the Scottish Vowel Length Rule, Liaison in French or Rendaku in Japanese, I have used upper case for the first letter.

ablaut A **process** in which a vowel in a **morpheme** changes to signal a **morpho-syntactic** property, as in the English pair *come* vs *came*, where the ablaut process signals past tense.

absolute neutralisation A form of **neutralisation** which was postulated in the history of **generative phonology**. It was characterised by the postulating of **underlying representations** which corresponded to none of the observed **surface forms**. For instance, in the analysis of Polish, some instances of phonetic [ɛ] **alternate with zero**, as in [pɔsɛł] vs [pɔsła], the nominative singular and genitive singular of the word for 'envoy', where we can see [ɛ] in the nominative form but no [ɛ] in the genitive form. These alternations are distinct from pairs such as [fɔtɛl] vs [fɔtɛla], the nominative singular and genitive singular forms of the word meaning 'armchair', where the [ɛ] does not alternate with zero. The suggestion is that the [ɛ]s which alternate with zero must be derived from an underlying representation other than /ɛ/. That underlying representation is said to be a **yer**, a non-**ATR** high vowel, represented as /ɨ/, which may be realised as [ɛ] or as zero. The objection raised to such analyses is that there is no phonetic [ɨ] in contemporary Polish, and that a child acquiring present-day Polish could not, therefore, possess mentally real underlying representations such as /ɨ/. Those who object to analyses involving absolute neutralisation point out that the yers existed in the history of Polish but no longer exist. To postulate such **abstract** representations for the **synchronic** phonology of Polish is arguably to represent **diachrony** mistakenly as **synchrony**. Most current versions of generative phonology are less abstract than those which adopted absolute neutralisation.

abstract This term is often used by phonologists to describe analyses in which phonological representations of words are postulated which are at some remove from the observable pronunciation of the word. A simple example is the phonological representation /wɪti/ of the word *witty* in **General American**. The normal pronunciation is [wɪɾi], with a **flap (tap)** rather than a [t]. Some phonologists claim that the flap results from a **synchronic process** of Flapping, in which the **phonemes** /t/ and /d/ are realised phonetically as an **alveolar** flap. See **realisation**. Phonological representations can be considerably more abstract than this. See **absolute neutralisation**. While some phonologists take the term 'abstract' to mean 'mentally real' in some sense, others who adopt **instrumentalism** intend 'abstract' to mean 'not corresponding to anything real outside of the theory'.

accent A term used, especially by British linguists, to identify varieties of a language with respect only to phonetic and phonological properties of that variety. Accent is often distinguished from **dialect**, which is said to denote, not just phonetic and phonological properties of a given variety, but also differences in vocabulary and syntax. An example of an accent of English is **Standard Scottish English** (SSE), which differs in its

vowel and consonant systems from the accent known as **Received Pronunciation** (also known as **Standard Southern British English**). For example, there is no /uː/ vs /ʊ/ contrast in SSE. An example of a dialect is Lowland Scots, whose syntax and vocabulary differ from the dialect known as Standard English. For example, 'ear' in Lowland Scots is 'lug', and 'chimney' is 'lum'. American linguists tend not to adopt the accent/dialect distinction.

The term 'accent' is also used as a synonym for **word stress**, so that an accented syllable is a stressed syllable.

active articulator The articulator which moves to form an articulation with a **passive articulator**. For example, in **alveolar** sounds, the **tip and/or the blade of the tongue** is the active articulator, and the **alveolar ridge** is the passive articulator; the tongue moves to form an articulation with the passive articulator.

Advanced Tongue Root (ATR) A property often associated with vowels, in which the **root** of the tongue is pushed forward, leading to various effects on the tongue **body**. Typical ATR and non-ATR vowel pairs are [i]/[ɪ], [u]/[ʊ], [e]/[ɛ], [o]/[ɔ]. **Low** vowels frequently fail to have an ATR counterpart, and often act as **opaque vowels** in ATR-based **vowel harmony** systems. ATR/non-ATR distinctions among **high** vowels often collapse during historical change, leaving only the ATR member, such as [i] or [u]. Such vowels often then act as **neutral vowels**.

affix A morphological unit attached to a **base**. The three main types of affix are prefixes, suffixes and infixes. Prefixes precede a base. Examples are the English prefix *un-*, as in *unhappy*, and the French prefix *re-*, as in *redemander* ('to ask again'). Suffixes follow a base. Examples are the English suffix *-ness*, as in *happiness*, and the French suffix *-ment*, as in *doucement* ('gently', from the adjective *douce*, meaning 'soft' or 'gentle'). Infixes are inserted inside a base. An example is the Tagalog infix *-um*, as in the word *sumulat*, which consists of the base *sulat* ('to write') with the infix *-um* inserted after the initial /s/.

affricate A type of speech sound involving a **stop** closure followed by slow release of the closure, resulting in audible friction, as in the case of the [tʃ] at the beginning and the end of the English word *church*.

airstream The flow of air on which speech sounds are based.

airstream mechanisms The various kinds of airstream which are harnessed in the production of human speech sounds. The one found in all human languages is the **pulmonic egressive** mechanism, in which air flows out from the lungs. A less common one is the **pulmonic ingressive** mechanism, in which air is sucked into the lungs. Sounds produced this way are called **implosives**. The **bilabial**, **alveolar** and **velar** implosives are transcribed as [ɓ], [ɗ] and [ɠ]. They are formed by making a **stop** closure in the oral cavity, sucking air into the lungs, releasing the closure, and allowing air to implode into the oral cavity. They are found in many African languages. Sounds produced with the **glottalic airstream mechanism** have a glottal closure and a stricture of complete closure made within the oral cavity. If the **larynx** is then raised, this pushes air upwards, creating an airstream, and if the oral closure is released, the air rushes out. Sounds made this way are called **ejectives**. The bilabial, alveolar and velar ejectives are transcribed as [p'], [t'] and [k']. These sounds are found in many American Indian languages. Sounds made with the **velaric airstream mechanism** have a closure between the **back of the tongue** and the **soft palate**, and another closure further forward in the oral cavity. If the velar closure is pulled back, this creates an ingressive airstream. This is the mechanism used in sucking. When the closure further forward in the oral cavity is released, air flows in. Sounds produced this way are called **clicks**. They are found in child **vocal play** and certain languages spoken mostly in Southern Africa, such as Zulu and Xhosa. The alveolar click is transcribed as [!] and the alveolar lateral click is transcribed as [ǁ]. The latter sound is used by speakers of various languages to 'gee-up' horses.

Aitken's Law see **Scottish Vowel Length Rule**

algorithm A set of **rules** or procedures. It is common to talk, for instance, of the algorithm for **word stress** assignment in a language. In Malay, the algorithm for word stress assignment is: place a **primary stress** on the **penultimate** syllable of the word, and then place a **secondary stress** on the initial syllable of the word and each alternate syllable thereafter, subject to **stress clash avoidance**.

allophone see **Phonemic Principle**

allophony The phenomenon whereby a **phoneme** has two or more **allophones**.

alternants Variant phonetic forms of a **morpheme**. The English morpheme *-in* has the alternant [ɪm] in *impossible*, [ɪn] in *indirect*, and [ɪŋ] in *incredible*. Such morpho-phonological alternations are **rule-governed**; in this case, the **place of articulation** of the **nasal stop** is determined by the place of articulation of the following consonant.

alternation The phenomenon whereby a **morpheme** has more than one **alternant**.

alveolar Sounds produced with the **alveolar ridge** as the **passive articulator** are alveolar sounds.

alveolar ridge The teeth ridge, located behind the upper teeth.

ambisyllabicity The boundary between **syllables** is often easy to establish, as in the French word *bateau* ('boat'): [ba.to]. But there are cases where there seems to be evidence for more than one possible syllabification. Take the English word *petrol*. On the one hand, the **Maximal Onset Principle** states that, since /tr/ is a legitimate **onset** cluster in English, the syllabification should be pe.trol. On the other hand, many speakers have a **glottal stop realisation** of the /t/ in this word, and for these speakers, /t/ is not normally realised as a glottal stop in onset position. Some phonologists have therefore suggested that in cases like this, the consonant in question is simultaneously in the **coda** of the **penultimate** syllable and in the onset of the final syllable; it is ambisyllabic, belonging to two syllables at the same time.

American Structuralism The kind of linguistics practised in the US in the 1930s, 1940s and 1950s, prior to the emergence of **generative phonology**. Names associated with this period include Leonard **Bloomfield**, Archibald Hill, Charles **Hockett**, Martin Joos, George

Trager and Rulon Wells. It is widely believed that the American Structuralists were sceptical about the existence of linguistic universals, unlike **Chomsky** and his followers. Like Chomsky, the American Structuralists believed that the kind of linguistics they practised was 'scientific', but their conception of what scientific method was differed radically from Chomsky's. Adopting a philosophy of science which was influenced by **logical positivism**, the American Structuralists assumed that genuinely scientific theories were based solely on observation and on **inductive generalisations** over those observations. Since the mind is unobservable, this meant excluding **mentalism** from linguistics. In the field of phonology, the American Structuralists are said to have postulated 'discovery procedures' by means of which the linguist can arrive at ('discover') the phonemic and morphophonemic system of a given language. Included in those 'discovery procedures' is the **Phonemic Principle**.

analogy A term used in psychology, linguistics and many other fields to refer to the human capacity to spot similarities between distinct objects or events. Some have said that there is an analogy between the Iraq War and the Vietnam War; they are said to be similar in certain respects. In phonology, it is often claimed that certain **diachronic** changes in languages are based on perceived analogies. The phenomenon known as **Intrusive 'r'** in **non-rhotic** varieties of English is often said to have come about by analogy with **Linking 'r'**. In child language acquisition, it has often been claimed that child forms such as *bringed* (instead of the irregular form *brought*) and *catched* (instead of *caught*) are formed by analogy with the past tense forms of regular verbs such as *banged* and *splashed*.

Anderson, John M. A Scottish linguist known, in syntax, for his work on case grammar and, in phonology, for the elaboration of the framework known as **Dependency Phonology**. Anderson is also known for his support of the Principle of **Structural Analogy**.

Anderson, Stephen R. An American linguist working in the **generative phonology** tradition, who has worked on a wide variety of phonological phenomena including **nasal** consonants, **tone**, **vowel harmony** and **metrical** structure. He is also a specialist in the history of phonology and is known for his theory of **morphology**.

antepenultimate Third last. Often used to refer to the position of a **syllable** in a word for the purposes of **word stress** assignment in languages where word stress is calculated from the end of the word.

anterior A distinctive **feature** used to differentiate different kinds of **coronal** speech sound types. Anterior coronals are **dental** or **alveolar** (such as [θ] and [s]), whereas **postalveolars**, such as [ʃ], are non-anterior.

antigemination A phenomenon whereby vowel **deletion** is blocked if it would lead to two identical adjacent consonants (i.e. a **geminate** consonant). In the Cushitic language Afar, unstressed vowels are deleted in the context #CVC_CV, so that /wager/ + /é/ ('he reconciled') becomes [wagré]. But the deletion fails to apply in cases such as /gonan/ + /a/ ('search for'), since the deletion would result in the sequence [gonna], with a geminate [nn].

apical Sounds made with the **tip of the tongue** are said to be apical. The **dental fricatives** [θ] and [ð] are examples.

apocope Loss of a **word-final segment**. This can be a **consonant** or a **vowel**. In English, word-final /t/ is often lost if the following word begins with a consonant, as in *last chance*: [lɑːstʃɑːns]. In Italian, the indefinite articles *uno* and *una* undergo loss of their final vowel if the following noun begins with a vowel, as in *una ragazza* ('a girl') vs *un' ora* ('an hour').

approximant see **degree of stricture**

archiphoneme A term used by **Prague School** phonologists such as **Trubetzkoy** when dealing with **neutralisation**. When the contrast between two **phonemes** in **opposition** is suspended (neutralised) in a specific context, one can postulate an archiphoneme, which is a representation of all of the properties shared by the phonemes in question. For instance, in Polish, there is a phonemic contrast between **voiced obstruents** and **voiceless** obstruents, but it is neutralised in word-final position, so that /trud/ ('labour') undergoes **Word-Final Devoicing** and is pronounced as [trut] in the singular. When the /d/ is not in word-final position, it is not **devoiced**, as in the plural form [trudi]. Trubetzkoy argued that what appears in word-final position is neither the voiced phoneme /d/ nor the voiceless phoneme /t/, but an archiphoneme /D/, which represents what the two phonemes have in common: they are both **stops** and are both **alveolar**.

Articulatory Phonetics That branch of **phonetics** which deals with the way human speech sounds are articulated.

Articulatory Phonology A phonological model which takes phonological representations to consist of sequences of overlapping phonological **gestures** such as **laryngeal** gestures and gestures in the **oral cavity**.

articulatory planning A term used to refer to the largely unconscious planning of the movements of the articulators during acts of uttering.

ash The name given to the vowel represented as /æ/ in work on the phonology of English. Ash is often a **low front unrounded** vowel, articulated somewhat higher than **cardinal vowel** 4.

aspiration Some phonologists argue that sounds which are aspirated are produced with spreading of the **vocal cords**. Others suggest that aspiration is produced by a delay in the onset of **voicing** after a stop closure has been released, as in the pronunciation [pʰɪt], in which it is claimed that there is a delay between the release of the **bilabial** stop closure and the onset of voicing for the following vowel [ɪ]. Aspirated stops are also sometimes referred to as **fortis** stops. See **Voice Onset Time**.

assimilation A **process** whereby two, normally adjacent, sounds become more similar to each other. An example of assimilation for **place of articulation** can be found in sequences such as *ten boys* in English, where the /n/ of *ten* tends to assimilate to the place of articulation of the following **bilabial** stop: [tʰɛmbɔɪz]. Assimilation for **voicing** is also common, as in the case of the **voiceless obstruents** of Hungarian, which become voiced when followed by another voiced obstruent, as seen in the root /kalap/ ('hat') which is realised with a voiced stop in [kalabban], where the suffix [ban] is added.

These examples involve **regressive (anticipatory) assimilation**, in which the first of two sounds assimilates to a following sound. This is the most common kind of assimilation, since it is **grounded** in **ease of** articulation. But **progressive (preservative) assimilation** is also attested, as in the case of the Lumasaaba morpheme /li/ ('a root') which is realised as [di] when a **nasal stop** precedes it, as in the form [zindi] ('roots'). Here, the complete closure of the nasal stop carries over on to the following sound, changing it from an **approximant** to a stop. In some cases, the sounds both preceding and following a segment can induce assimilation. This is what happens with **intervocalic voicing**, as in the case of voiceless unaspirated stops in Korean, which are realised as voiced stops intervocalically: /pap/ ('cooked rice') is realised with a [b] when the suffix /i/ is added: [pabi]. There are also cases of **reciprocal assimilation**, in which each of the adjacent sounds assimilates to the other, as in the case of *Raise your hand!* in English, typically uttered as [ɹeɪʒəhænd]. In this case, the [z] at the end of *raise* becomes a **postalveolar** [ʒ] under the influence of the palatal glide /j/ at the beginning of *your*, and the **palatal** glide becomes a [ʒ] as a result of progressive assimilation. Reciprocal assimilation is also known as **coalescence**. Some phonologists claim that long-distance assimilation exists, in which the **segments** in question are not adjacent. Examples of this are the phenomena known as **consonant harmony** and **vowel harmony**.

atonic vowel An unstressed **vowel**. In the Latin word *amare* ('to love'), the final vowel is an atonic vowel. See **tonic vowel** and **countertonic vowel**.

ATR see **Advanced Tongue Root**

auditory phonetics That branch of **phonetics** which deals with the way that the human ear and perceptual system receive and process speech sounds.

Autosegmental Phonology A way of depicting, and conceiving of, phonological representation which departed from previous purely **segmental** models of phonological structure and postulated several tiers of phonological structure. For **tone languages**, a tonal tier was postulated on which tones were represented as autosegments, overlaid on a sequence of segments, as in the following diagram:

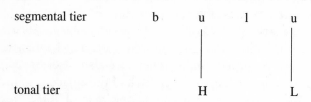

segmental tier   b   u   l   u

tonal tier   H   L

Here, 'H' and 'L' represent **high** and **low** tones.

The same approach came to be applied to certain languages with **nasal harmony**. A nasal autosegment was postulated, located on a nasal tier. The nasal autosegment was then said to be able to attach to individual segments, which would then be nasal consonants or **nasalised** vowels, as in Gokana [nũ] ('thing'), represented as:

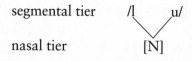

segmental tier   /l   u/

nasal tier   [N]

where '[N]' represents a nasal autosegment which gets attached to the segments on the segmental tier. Autosegmental Phonology is a form of **non-linear phonology**. It has been suggested by some that **Firthian Phonology** was a historical precursor of Autosegmental Phonology, since Firthian **prosodies** seem parallel to autosegments.

avoidance of homophony It is believed by some that there is a general trend towards avoiding the application of phonological **processes** which create **homophones**, since we need to maintain lexical contrasts for functional reasons; if most of the **minimal pairs** of a language were to become homophones, the language would be less useful for purposes of communication.

In the history of French, the Latin word *gallus* ('cockerel/rooster') underwent a sound change whereby the **intervocalic** /l/ became a /t/, resulting in forms such as *gattus*, which is homophonous with the Latin word *gattus*, meaning 'cat'. In this case, homophony was avoided by using an alternative name for a cockerel, resulting in the present-day word *coq*.

B

babbling A phenomenon which begins during the second half of the first year of life, following, but overlapping with, the **vocal play** period, in which the child utters **syllable**-like sequences, based on rhythmic movements of the jaw. The syllables in question are often of the CV (consonant-vowel) type, such as [da]. When the child utters **reduplicated** sequences of identical syllables, such as [dadada], this is referred to as **canonical babbling**. When the child utters sequences of non-identical syllables, such as [bada], this is referred to as **variegated babbling**. The amount of variegated babbling increases towards the end of the first year of life. Unfortunately, some writers use the term babbling to refer to the pre-babbling vocalisations of the vocal play period.

back see **features**

back of the tongue That part of the **body of the tongue**, behind the **front of the tongue** and in front of the **tongue root**, which is the **active articulator** in **velar** and **uvular** sounds.

backing see **vowel retraction**

base A term used in **morphology**, to denote any part of a word to which an **affix** may be added. In the English word *unhappy*, the base is *happy*. This is the kind of base known as a **root**. Roots contain no affixes. The base in *friendliness* is *friendly*. In this case, the base is not a root; it contains the morphemes *friend* and *-ly*.

Baudouin de Courtnay, Jan (1845–1929) Baudouin worked in Russia and later in his native Poland. He was part of the **Kazan School**. His work influenced the thinking of the **Prague School**. Baudouin distinguished between the purely physical aspects of sound structure, which he called anthropophonics, and the psychological aspect of sound systems, which he called psychophonetics. This is a **phonetics/phonology** distinction in which phonology (psychophonetics) is seen as **mentalistic** phonetics. Baudouin also elaborated a theory of **alternations** and a theory of **phonologisation** in which alternations start out as phonetically grounded, but that grounding can become obscured in the course of time, leading to **opacity**.

BBC English Another term for **Received Pronunciation**.

Behaviourism A particularly extreme form of **Empiricism** practised in the mid-twentieth century, in which it was held that only observable behaviour constitutes the object of a properly scientific linguistics. Behaviourism is thus fundamentally opposed to any variety of **mentalism**, since the contents of the mind are, by definition, unobservable. It is associated with the work of B. F. Skinner and Leonard **Bloomfield**. It is important to bear in mind that, if one allows that both observable behaviour and mental realities constitute the object of linguistic (and thus phonological) inquiry, that does not constitute Behaviourism.

bilabial see **labial**

bilateral opposition see **opposition**

bimoraic see **mora**

binary-valued features see **feature values**

bisyllabic Containing two **syllables,** as in the French word *bateau*: [ba.to]. The term **disyllabic** is a synonym.

blade That part of the tongue just behind the **tip,** usually involved in **alveolar** articulations.

blockers see **opaque vowels** and **nasal spread**

Bloomfield, Leonard (1887–1949) An American linguist who worked on the native languages of North America and who is often associated with **American Structuralism**. Influenced by the drift away from **mentalism** in psychology, Bloomfield adopted, not only **Empiricism,** but also **Behaviourism**. Because he opposed mentalism, Bloomfield argued that one should analyse linguistic structure independently of meaning, but he inevitably failed to do so. Bloomfield embraced the concept of the **phoneme,** but one cannot establish phonemic contrasts without recourse to meaning (see **minimal pairs**). Bloomfield believed that linguistics could be 'scientific', and his conception of what this meant was influenced by **logical positivism**. It is because of this conception that he believed that the only scientifically valid generalisations in linguistics were **inductive generalisations**.

Boas, Franz (1858–1942) A German linguist who became an American citizen in the late nineteenth century. Associated with anthropological linguistics in the USA, in which language is viewed as a set of cultural practices, Boas engaged in a great deal of fieldwork on the native languages of the North American Indians. His best-known student was Edward **Sapir**.

body of the tongue The main part of the tongue, excluding the **tip**, **blade** and **root**.

bootstrapping problem A problem in child language acquisition. The problem is this: if the child decodes speech by mapping utterances of words on to words stored in the child's mind, how can the child make a start? In order to have mental representations of words stored in the mind, the child must first extract words from the stream of speech. But how can the child extract these if he/she does not already have mental representations of words? There are not normally pauses between words in the stream of speech, so how is the child to know which sequences of phonetic **segments** constitute words? One response to this puzzle is to appeal to the child's capacity to extract statistical tendencies from the stream of speech (see **stochastic phonology**). The term 'bootstrapping' may come from the expression 'to pull oneself up by one's own bootstraps', meaning to get started from scratch without help, or from its application to computers, which have a bootstrapping program which gets the computer started when it is switched on.

borrowing see **loanword**. The term is also used in the literature on **code-switching**, to denote words uttered by bilinguals which have been taken from one of the speaker's languages and phonologically or morphologically modified in accordance with the system of the other language. An utterance such as *L'ordinateur est disconnecté* ('The computer is disconnected'), uttered by a bilingual speaker, contains the English word *disconnected* which is borrowed and modified, both phonologically and morphologically, to fit with the phonology and morphology of French. The phonological modification lies in the utterance of the English prefix *dis-* as [dis], with a French [i] vowel instead of an English [ɪ] vowel. The morphological modification lies in the uttering of the French suffix *-é* instead of the English suffix *-ed*.

boundary tone The tone that occurs at the edge of an **intonation group**. The notion is used by phonologists who analyse intonation contours by separating them into their component tones. Boundary tones are represented in the representational system **ToBI**.

branching onset An **onset** which contains more than one **consonant**, as in the English word *brow*. The term 'branching' derives from the use of **tree diagrams** to represent **syllable** structure; a branching onset is visually represented using a diagram in which the onset **node** contains two branches.

breaking A synonym for **diphthongisation**.

broad Used to describe **non-standard accents** which have not been influenced by features of standard accents. Accents may be more or less broad; the broader the accent, the more non-standard features it retains. Thus, a speaker with a broad Liverpool English accent will retain all of the features of that non-standard accent, such as the **lenition** of **voiceless stops** to **affricates** or **fricatives**, as in [bʊx] for *book*. This is one of the few terms to be used, in much the same sense, by specialists and the general public alike.

broad transcription Usually defined in contradistinction to **narrow transcription**. The difference between the two is that, the narrower a transcription, the more phonetic detail it contains. Broader transcriptions contain less phonetic detail and often approximate to **phonemic transcription**. Some authors equate broad transcription with phonemic transcription.

Bybee, Joan Under the name Joan Hooper, this American phonologist was associated with **Natural Generative Phonology** and has more recently been associated with **usage-based phonology**.

C

C Stands for **consonant**. For example, when phonologists speak of **CV syllables**, they mean simple syllables with a single consonant in the **onset** position and a single vowel in the **nucleus** position.

canonical babbling see **babbling**

cardinal vowels Specific **vowel qualities** which are used as reference points for locating any given vowel articulation. The cardinal vowel system of description is based on the idea that one can distinguish the **high-low** dimension from the **front-back** dimension. The cardinal vowels are often said to be vowel qualities produced at certain very peripheral points in the **vowel space**, such as cardinal vowel 1, which is said to be produced with the tongue as high and as far front as it can go in the mouth without friction being created (and with the lips **unrounded**). It has often been claimed that, in making the transition from, say, cardinal vowel 1 ([i]) through cardinal vowel 2 ([e]), to cardinal vowel 3 ([ɛ]) and on to cardinal vowel 4 ([a]), the **body of the tongue** descends through a series of equidistant steps. But it has equally often been pointed out that this seems not to be physiologically true. None the less, the cardinal vowel system of representing vowel qualities in a trapezium-shaped chart is still seen as a useful, practical way of visualising the vowel space and the available range of vowel qualities. The cardinal vowel chart is still used in the **International Phonetic Alphabet**.

categorisation The act of allocating specific objects and events to categories. This can range from categorising a given object as an instance of, say, a spoon, to the categorisation of a given speech sound to a particular category. In decoding the speech signal, humans are able to allocate a given speech sound to a specific speech sound **type**; we can hear a given speech sound as an instance of a [t] or an [s], for example. Many believe that categorisation is central to perception. See **normalisation**.

Celtic A **language family** which subsumes present-day languages such as Scots Gaelic, Irish Gaelic, Welsh and Breton. Part of the **Indo-European language family**.

central The area of the **vowel space** between **front** and **back**. Front vowels lie below the **hard palate**, back vowels lie below the **velum** (soft palate), and central vowels lie below where the two meet. An example of a central vowel is the high, **rounded** 'u'-type sound produced in Scottish English; transcribed as [ʉ], it lies between high back [u] and high front [y]. The term is also used, in the description of consonants, for sounds in which the air escapes down a groove in the tongue. Most of the **fricatives** and **approximants** in English have central escape of air, as in the **alveolar** fricative [s]. See **lateral**.

centralisation A vowel articulation is said to be centralised if it is produced closer to the central area of the **vowel space** than it might otherwise have been. In the **IPA**, centralised vowels are transcribed with a dieresis, as in [ë], which denotes a centralised version of the **cardinal vowel** [e]. An example of a centralised vowel in English is the [ë] of Scottish English, a centralised version of [ɛ] found in many Scottish speakers' pronunciation of the stressed vowel in words such as *eleven, seven, next, yesterday*.

centring diphthong A **diphthong** in which a transition is made towards the centre of the **vowel space**, in the area where **schwa** is produced. The **RP** centring diphthongs are [ɪə], [ʊə] and [ɛə], as in *here, poor* and *there*.

checked syllable Synonym for a **closed syllable**.

checked vowel Another name for the set of English vowels which are known as **short** or **lax** vowels.

Chomsky, Noam An American linguist who has worked in the second half of the twentieth century and in the early twenty-first century. His name is closely associated with **generative linguistics**. In the field of **phonology**, he co-authored *The Sound Pattern of English* (**SPE**) with Morris **Halle,** thus establishing the framework known as **SPE phonology,** widely seen as the starting point for **generative phonology**. He is known for advocating **Rationalism** in linguistics.

clash avoidance see **stress clash avoidance**

Classical Latin The standard language spoken in Ancient Rome, Latin was imposed on the inhabitants of the Roman Empire, and was used as a **lingua franca** among scholars throughout Europe for centuries after the demise of the Roman Empire. Classical Latin is usually distinguished from **Vulgar Latin,** the version of Latin spoken by the lay person, by colonising Roman soldiers and by merchants. It is Vulgar Latin that is taken to be the source from which the present-day **Romance languages** evolved.

'**clear l**' This term could be used to denote a **lateral** that is **palatalised,** as in the 'l' sound found in the Scottish English of the Highlands of Scotland, in words such as [lʲʌlʲ] (*lull*), where the superscript **diacritic** 'ʲ' denotes palatalisation. One would then have three main types of 'l': '**dark l**', 'clear l', and an 'l' which is neither clear nor dark (neither **velarised** nor palatalised). However, the term is used to refer to 'l' sounds which are not palatalised, but are also not pronounced with a **retraction** of the **body of the tongue**; they are not 'dark l's'. In **Received Pronunciation** (RP), the /l/ phoneme is realised as a 'dark l' in the **rhyme** of **syllables,** but it is not 'dark' in **onset** position. Many authors refer to this 'non-dark' l as 'clear l'.

Clements, Nick An American phonologist with French (and British) connections who has worked in the USA. Since 1992, the leader of a phonology research team in Paris, he has worked extensively in both the **generative phonology** tradition and in the **Laboratory Phonology** community. He is a specialist in the phonology of various African languages who has worked on, among other things, **nasality**, distinctive **features** in the world's languages, **feature geometry**, **tone** and the phonetics/phonology **interface**.

clicks see **airstream mechanisms**

clitic A unit which is intermediate between a word and an **affix**, as in the French pronouns *je*, *te* and *le* in *Je te le rends* ('I'm giving it back to you'), which do not seem to have the status of full words such as *livre* in *Je te rends ton livre*. Nor do they seem to have the same status as affixes, such as the prefix *re-* in *redemander* ('ask again'). Such units are not affixes, but they are unlike full words in that they typically do not receive the **tonic accent** in an **intonation group**. They also undergo **reduction processes**, such as the **elision** of the **schwa** vowel, often conveyed in spelling via the use of apostrophes, as in *J't'aime* ('I love you'), pronounced [ʃtɛm]. In English, units such as the *n't* in expressions like *couldn't* are said to be clitics. A clitic which follows its 'host' (such as *n't*) is called an **enclitic**. A clitic which precedes its 'host' (such as the *J'* and the *t'* in *J't'aime*) is called a **proclitic**.

cliticisation A **process** in which full words are 'demoted' to the status of **clitics**. In the expression *wannabe*, from *want to be*, the words *to* and *be* are 'fused' with *want* to form a single **trochaic foot** which may then function as a single word.

close approximation see **degree of stricture**

close juncture see **juncture**

closed syllable see **syllable**

coalescence A **process** in which two sounds **assimilate** to each other. In English, a sequence of **alveolar** [s] followed by the **palatal approximant** [j] will often result in coalescence, yielding the **palato-alveolar** sound [ʃ], as in [mɪʃə] for *miss you*. Also known as **reciprocal assimilation**.

Cockney The popular term for **broad** varieties of **London English**.

coda see **syllable**

code-switching A phenomenon found among both adult and child bilinguals, in which the speaker switches from one language to another during a single sentence or **intonation group**. This is relevant for phonological investigation, since such speakers switch from one phonological system to another during a single utterance.

cognition Mental states and processes.

cognitive Relating to **cognition**. Those who support a cognitive view of phonology argue that phonology is about investigating certain mental states and processes, such as phonological representations understood as representations in the mind. On this view, the study of phonological representations and **processes** is a part of **cognitive science**.

cognitive science The science of mental states and processes. Many believe that it is possible to gain scientific understanding of at least some aspects of the human mind.

compensatory lengthening A **process** in which a **segment** undergoes **elision** and an adjacent segment lengthens. Very often, it is a **coda** consonant which is elided, and a preceding vowel is lengthened. In the history of French, vowel + /s/ + consonant sequences underwent elision of the /s/ and compensatory lengthening of the preceding vowel, as in the transition from **Old French** *beste* ('beast'), pronounced [bɛstə], to a later form with an elided /s/ and a lengthened /ɛ/: [bɛːtə], reflected in the present-day spelling *bête*, where the circumflex historically marked the length of the vowel.

competence A term associated with the work of Noam Chomsky and thus widely used in **generative linguistics**. It designates a speaker's linguistic knowledge, as opposed to the use of that knowledge. Most generative linguists assume that there is a phonological component within a speaker's linguistic competence. It is important to bear in mind that, in speaking of linguistic competence, Chomsky is using an everyday term in a specialist sense. In everyday language, 'competence' means ability to do something well, ability to perform certain tasks to a certain level. Chomsky denies that knowing a language is knowing how to do something. See **I-language**, **E-language** and **performance**.

complement A term used in syntax to refer to obligatory syntactic **constituents**, as in the noun phrase *the dog* in the sentence *John kicked the dog*. In this example, the noun phrase *the dog* is said to be the complement of the verb *kicked*. The verb *kicked*, being a transitive verb, must be followed by a complement, in this case known as a direct object. Phonologists who postulate parallelisms between syntactic structure and phonological structure have argued that certain phonological constituents are complements. For instance, **coda** consonants are said by some to be complements of the vowels which precede them, as in the word /kæt/ (*cat*), where the coda consonant /t/ is said to be the complement of the vowel /æ/; the **nucleus** of the syllable is said to require a complement in the form of a coda consonant. Frameworks which have adopted the notion of complement in phonology include **Dependency Phonology**, **Government Phonology** and **Head-Driven Phonology**.

complementary distribution see **Phonemic Principle**

complete closure see **degree of stricture**

complex segment Another term for a **contour segment**.

compound A word made from two or more other words. Simple two-part cases in English include words such as *textbook*, *eyelid* and *mole-hill*. Many phonologists postulate a compound stress rule for English in which the first of the two elements is the most prominent. But there are large numbers of English two-part compounds in which the second element is the most prominent. The criteria for establishing whether a given sequence of two words in English is a phrase or a compound include both phonological and semantic phenomena.

concrete A term often used to describe postulated phonological representations which are said to be close to the phonetic form of words as they are pronounced by speakers. It is often opposed to **abstract**. The distinction is closely related to the difficult problem of the possible distinction between **phonology** and **phonetics**. See **realisation**.

Connectionism see **neural nets**

consonant Consonants are a subset of the set of human speech sounds. Consonants are produced with three different **degrees of stricture: complete closure, close approximation** and **open approximation**. Consonants can be defined in terms of their position in **syllable** structure; they usually occupy the **onset** and **coda** positions, whereas **vowels** occupy the **head** of the **nucleus** position in a syllable (but see **syllabic consonants**). Some consonants, such as the **glides** [w] and [j], often called **semiconsonants**, share with vowels a stricture of open approximation, but, unlike vowels, do not occupy the head of the syllable nucleus. There is a continuum among the set of human speech sounds from most consonantal to most vowel-like. See **sonority hierarchy**.

consonant harmony In child speech, a phenomenon in which a **consonant** is altered so as to harmonise with, i.e. become more similar to, another consonant, as in [wɪpu] for 'whistle', where a **coronal** sound (the [s]) in the adult target is uttered as a **labial** ([p]), thus harmonising with the initial labial (the [w]). The harmonising consonant may become identical to another consonant, as in [gɒg] or [dɒd] for 'dog'. Child consonant harmony usually involves **major place of articulation**. There is a general tendency for coronals to cede place of articulation to non-coronals, as in [wɪpu] and [gɒg], but the reverse is attested, as in [dɒd]. Individual children vary a great deal in the extent to which they produce harmonised forms. There is also variation in the shape of words which undergo consonant harmony. For instance, some individual children will have harmony in CVC and CVCVC words, but not in CVCV words.

In adult phonology, consonant harmony for major place of articulation is unattested, but there are many phenomena involving harmony for **minor place of articulation**, as in Navajo **sibilant harmony**, where the **underlying representation** /j-iʃ-mas/ (I'm rolling along') becomes [jismas], with the **palato-alveolar** /ʃ/ harmonising with the **alveolar** /s/.

consonant system see **Phonemic Principle**

consonant vocalisation A **process** whereby a **consonant** articulation becomes **vowel**-like. In **London English**, an /l/ in the **rhyme** of a **syllable** is frequently realised as a [w] sound, as in [gɛw] for 'girl', where the /l/ is in **coda** position.

consonantal Pertaining to **consonants**; consonant-like. The term is also used as a **distinctive feature**.

conspiracy Two or more distinct phonological **processes** can 'conspire' to bring about a specific pattern. In Swedish, the plural ending for nouns is *-or*. When this is added to a noun **root** ending in a vowel, the final vowel of the root deletes, so that when the plural suffix is added to a root such as *flicka*, the resulting form is *flickor*, with **deletion** of the *-a*. The definite article in Swedish is the suffix *-an*. When this is added to a root ending in a vowel, the /a/ in the suffix is deleted, so that *flicka* becomes *flickan*. These are distinct processes, but they 'conspire' to block sequences of two vowels across a **morpheme boundary**.

constituent A term used in both syntax and phonology. In syntax, it denotes a set of words which go together to form a structural unit. In the sentence *Jim is in the park*, the sequence *in the park* forms a constituent known as a prepositional phrase. In phonology, **syllables** are often said to be composed of the two main constituents **onset** and **rhyme**. Phonologists also postulate **metrical** constituents of words and phrases, the main such constituent being the metrical **foot**.

constraint A way of stating an observed generalisation. Examples are **phonotactic constraints**, which are ways of stating which sequences of **segments** may occur in specific parts of a **syllable** in a given language (for instance, the **onset** sequence /pn/ violates English phonotactic constraints). In the history of **generative phonology**, a transition occurred in the 1990s from the **SPE** tradition, which postulated both **rules** and constraints, to **Optimality Theory**, which attempts to state all phonological generalisations in terms of constraints. The notion of 'constraint' is essentially more **declarative** than the notion of rule, which is easily interpreted as **process**. Constraints also play a central role in the Theory of Constraints and Repair Strategies proposed by Carole **Paradis**.

constricted glottis A **feature** used to denote the closure of the **vocal cords** found in **glottal stops** and **glottalised** sounds.

constriction Synonym for stricture. See **degree of stricture**.

constructivism An approach to child language acquisition which takes the child to be actively constructing his/her linguistic knowledge. In the field of child syntax, a well-known constructivist is Michael **Tomasello**. In the field of child phonology, the work of Marilyn **Vihman** is constructivist. In the field of developmental disorders in child language acquisition, Annette **Karmiloff-Smith**'s work is constructivist. Constructivists reject the Chomskyan conception of the child's linguistic development.

content word Another term for words of a **lexical category**.

contour segment A segment in which there are two distinct subparts, occurring in sequence. **Affricates** are often said to be contour segments, since they consist of a **stop** closure followed by a **fricative** release. **Prenasalised stops** are also often analysed as contour segments. **Pre-aspirated stops** in some languages may be analysed this way too.

contrastive function see **phoneme**

contrastive stress A term used to refer to the placement of **tonics** to highlight a contrast. The 'neutral' or unmarked **tonic placement** in the sentence *John went to the pub* would have the tonic on *pub*, since it is the **last lexical item**. But if one were seeking to emphasise the fact that it was John, and not someone else, who went to the pub, one could place the tonic on *John*, thus contrasting John with some other person. The terms 'contrastive **intonation**' or 'contrastive tonic placement' would seem more appropriate than 'contrastive stress'.

cooing A term used by some child phonology experts to describe the first comfort sounds, uttered in the 2–4-month age period. These sounds are normally produced in response to adults smiling at and talking to the child.

corner vowels The four corner points in the **cardinal vowel** chart: cardinal vowel 1 ([i]), 4 ([a]), 5 ([ɑ]) and 8 ([u]).

coronal A term used to subsume **dental, alveolar** and **postalveolar** consonants, which are all produced using the **blade** of the tongue. The word has the same root as *crown* and *coronation* but, for some reason, we speak of the *blade*, rather than the *crown*, of the tongue. Various theories of **distinctive features** make use of [coronal] as a feature.

correlate A term used to denote the relationship between some phonological phenomenon and its phonetic **realisation**. It is often said, for example, that the phonetic correlates of **word stress** are increased **duration**, increased loudness, or **pitch** movement. Some languages rely more on pitch movement than duration to signal word stress, while others rely equally on both.

The term is used as a verb in work on **sociophonetic variation**. We may say, for example, that occurrence of **pre-aspirated** [t] in **Tyneside English** correlates with age, social class and gender, since it is used mostly by young working-class women.

correlation In **sociophonetic** inquiry, it is common to try to establish whether a given **sociolinguistic parameter**, such as age or social class, correlates with the presence of a given pronunciation feature, such as **non-rhotic**

speech. In **New York City English**, degree of non-rhoticity correlates with the social class of the speaker.

countertonic vowel A vowel which receives **secondary stress**. In **Classical Latin** and **Vulgar Latin**, word-initial vowels which did not bear **primary stress** received a secondary stress, as in the word *amare* ('to love'), in which the initial vowel is the countertonic vowel and the second vowel receives primary stress. See **tonic vowel**.

creole When children are exposed to a **pidgin** language as their first language during the language acquisition period, the language becomes less simplified than the pidgin. This **process** is known as creolisation.

creolisation see **creole**

CV syllable A **syllable** consisting of a single **consonant** in the **onset** position and a single vowel in the **nucleus**, with no **coda** consonant. Syllables of this sort are often assumed to be the most basic, or simple, sorts of syllable. They are found universally in the **babbling** stage of child development. Some languages have **phonotactic constraints** which allow only CV syllables.

$\boxed{\text{D}}$

'dark l' An informal term used to denote a **lateral** that has a **secondary articulation** involving the **body of the tongue**, usually the **back of the tongue**, which may form a structure of **open approximation** with the **velum**, resulting in **velarisation** of the lateral. Some 'dark l' sounds may have a **retraction** of the body of the tongue which is not raised towards the velum, but is withdrawn towards the back of the **oral cavity**, without being raised. The British **accent** referred to as **Received Pronunciation** (RP) has 'dark l' in the **rhyme** of **syllables**, but not in the **onset** position in syllables, as can be seen in the RP pronunciation of words such as *lull*: [lʌɫ]. Here, the /l/ in the onset position is not dark, but the /l/ in **coda** position of the rhyme is a 'dark l'. See '**clear l**'.

declarative A distinction is often made between an essentially static way of conceiving of phonological generalisations, and an essentially dynamic way of stating those generalisations. The static way involves stating what the well-formed phonological structures are in a given language (**phonotactic constraints** are an example). This kind of approach is said to be declarative. The dynamic way leans on the notion of phonological **processes**, such as the idea of **syllabification** processes which actively build syllable structure.

declarative phonology A phonological model is declarative if it states phonological generalisations in such a way as to avoid any appeal to the notion of **derivation**. It is sometimes claimed, in models which are said to be declarative, that phonological representations in those models are more **concrete** than those in derivational models, in that the phonological representations postulated in declarative models are said to represent **surface forms** 'directly'.

declination see **downdrift**

default A term used to denote an **unmarked** state of affairs. The placement of the **tonic** in English on the **last lexical item** is the default placement. Default values of **features** are the values that are supplied to

underspecified representations if no **process** has applied to provide a non-default value. The unmarked voicing state for **sonorants** in human languages is that they are **voiced**. Some phonologists have therefore postulated default rules to supply feature [voiced] to sonorants, which are left unspecified for voicing state in **underlying representations**.

degemination A **process** in which a **geminate segment** is simplified to become non-geminate. In the English word *immaterial*, the prefix *in-* is added to the adjective *material*. But the word is pronounced with a non-geminate [m]: [ɪmə'tɪəɹiəl], and not as [ɪmmə'tɪəɹiəl], with a **fake geminate**. This is in contrast to words such as *unnatural*, where degemination does not take place; the prefix *un-* is added to the root *natural*, resulting in the pronunciation [ʌn'nætʃəɹəl], with a fake geminate.

degree of stricture The extent to which airflow is obstructed in the production of a sound. Three degrees of stricture are often recognised. **Complete closure** represents the highest degree of stricture: the airflow is blocked completely. Sounds produced this way are called **stops** or **plosives**. Examples are the [p] in *open*, the [t] in *butter* and the [k] in *bucket*. **Close approximation** constitutes a less extreme degree of stricture: the articulators come into close contact, but the airflow is not completely blocked. Rather, it escapes through a small space, causing turbulence, heard as audible friction. Sounds produced this way are called **fricatives**. Examples are the [θ] in *thin*, the [f] in *fin*, the [s] in *sin* and the [ʃ] in *shin*. **Open approximation** is an even less extreme degree of stricture: the articulators do not come close enough to cause friction. Sounds produced this way are called **approximants** and **vowels**. Examples are the approximants [j] and [w] in *yes* and *go*, and the vowels [iː] and [ɑː] in *see* and *far* in certain varieties of English. Degree of stricture is also known as **manner of articulation.**

deletion A term used to refer to the loss (**elision**) of a **segment** or **syllable.**

Dell, François A French phonologist who works in the tradition of **generative phonology**. In the early 1970s, Dell approached the phonology of French from the perspective of **SPE phonology**. He is also known for his later work on the phonology of the Berber language. With Nick **Clements**, he runs a phonology research laboratory in Paris.

dental Sounds which are dental involve an articulation between the **tip of the tongue** and the upper teeth. An example is the **voiceless** dental **fricative** at the end of the English word *teeth*: [tiːθ]. Dental **stops** are also widely attested, as in the pronunciation [t̪ʰɪŋ] for *thing*, where the subscript **diacritic** indicates that the articulation is dental. This phenomenon is attested in many varieties of English. See **TH-Stopping.**

depalatalisation A **process** whereby **palatal** sounds become non-palatal, usually as a result of a process of **assimilation**. In Polish, the palatal phonemes /ć/, /j́/ and /ń/ are realised as alveolar [t], [d] and [n] respectively when followed by **coronal segments,** as in the **morpheme** /vilgoć/ ('moisture') which is realised with a [t] in the adjective [vilgotnɨ] ('moist').

Dependency Phonology A framework associated with the linguist John M. **Anderson,** in which the **head**-dependent relation is central. Dependency Phonology uses **elements**, rather than binary-valued **features**, in the characterisation of **segmental** structure. Dependency relations are postulated to hold between **elements** within segments, between the **constituents** within a **syllable**, and between the syllables within a **foot**. In this framework, elements cluster together to form **gestures**.

dependent see **head**

derivation Models of phonological organisation which posit more than one level of **representation**, and which map one level on to another, contain appeal to the notion of a derivation, in which one level is derived from the other. A simple example would be a **phonemic** model in which the **phonetic** level is derived from the phonemic level, as in the derivation of the phonetic representation [pʰʊɫ] from the phonemic representation /pʊl/ (*pull*). **SPE phonology** is derivational, since it appeals to the idea of postulating two levels of representation (**underlying representations** and **surface forms**) and deriving one from the other, often via the ordered application of a set of **rules**.

derivational phonology Any model of phonology which appeals to the notion of a **derivation**. An example is **SPE phonology**.

derived see **derivation**

derived contrast One often finds **minimal pairs** in which one member of the pair is **morphologically complex**, while the other is not. In Northern Irish English, the /e/ phoneme often has an [eə] **allophone** in **closed syllables**, as in *same* and *daze*: [seəm] and [deəz]. It often has an [ɛː] allophone in **open syllables**, as in *day*: [dɛː]. When one adds the plural suffix to nouns such as *day*, the pronunciation tends to retain the [ɛː] allophone of the singular: [dɛːz] (*days*), despite the fact that the vowel is in a closed syllable in *days*. One thus finds minimal pairs such as [deəz] (*daze*) vs [dɛːz] (*days*). Such contrasts are often referred to as derived contrasts; the contrast is derived from a morphological **process** (here, the addition of the plural suffix). Such contrasts seem distinct from non-derived contrasts such as [get] (*gate*) and [gɛt] (*get*). Also known as **marginal contrasts**. See **paradigm uniformity effect**.

devoicing A **process** in which an underlyingly **voiced** phoneme is realised as **voiceless**. Final devoicing involves the devoicing of voiced **obstruents** in **word-final** or syllable-final position, as in the German word [ʁat] ('wheel'), which is underlyingly /ʁad/, as seen in the form [ʁadəs] ('of the wheel'). Consonants may be devoiced because they are adjacent to a voiceless sound, as in the case of the French voiced **uvular fricative** /ʁ/, which is devoiced in **onset** clusters when preceded by a voiceless **stop**. The French word *train* ('train') is /tʁɛ̃/ phonologically, but [tχɛ̃] phonetically, with a voiceless uvular fricative. This latter kind of devoicing is a form of **assimilation**.

diachronic Relating to **diachrony**. The diachronic phonology of a language is the study of how its phonology has changed during its history.

diachrony From the Ancient Greek meaning 'through time'. Studies in the diachrony of a language are studies of the way it has changed over time. Opposed to synchrony.

diacritic A visual symbol used in transcriptions to denote some phonetic property. An example is the 'ʰ' diacritic used to denote **aspiration** in **voiceless stops**, as in the English word *tip*: [tʰɪp]. Some diacritics are superscript diacritics, such as the one we have just seen; they are written above the relevant symbol. Others are subscript diacritics; they are placed below the relevant symbol, as in the case of the diacritic for **Advanced Tongue Root**: [e̞] denotes an [e] with ATR. Some diacritics run through the symbols in question, as in the case of the **velarisation** diacritic used to represent 'dark l' and other velarised sounds; *full* in English is often transcribed as [fʊɫ], although the **IPA** now represents velarised consonants with a superscript diacritic: [fʊlˠ]

dialect see **accent**

diphthong A vowel sound in which there is a transition from one **vowel quality** to another within a single syllable **nucleus**, as in the English word [baɪ] (*buy*). Transitions from one vowel quality to another across syllable boundaries are not diphthongs; English [siːɪŋ] (*seeing*) has a transition from [iː] to [ɪ], but this is not a diphthong, since the transition does not take place within a single nucleus.

diphthongisation A **process** in which a **monophthong** becomes a **diphthong**. For example, the monophthongs /e/ and /o/ have undergone diphthongisation in many varieties of English to become, for example, [eɪ] and [əʊ]. Referred to informally as **breaking**.

Direct Syntax Hypothesis A claim that syntactic structure may directly affect phonological **processes**. Some have argued, for instance, that **Liaison** in French is triggered by sequences of words which form a close syntactic unit, as in *les amis* ('the friends'): [lezami], in which the **latent consonant** is pronounced since the definite article and the noun form a syntactic **constituent**.

disharmony Many languages which have **vowel harmony** contain words with vowels from different harmonic sets, as in Hungarian [sofør] 'driver', which has a vowel from the **back** set and a vowel from the **front** set. Such cases are often **loanwords**, as is the case here, where the word is from French *chauffeur* ([ʃofœʁ]). Disharmony can also be induced by the presence of **neutral vowels** and **opaque vowels**.

Dispersion Theory The claim that vowel **phonemes** tend to be dispersed across the **vowel space**. The idea is that, the fewer the vowel contrasts in a given language, the more unlike each other the vowels will be, so that a language with, say, only three vowel phonemes will have maximally distinct **vowel qualities**, typically /i/, /u/ and /a/, rather than, say, /i/, /e/ and /ɛ/. This minimal **vowel triangle** plays a central role in element-based theories such as **Dependency Phonology**. The three vowels in question are sometimes referred to as the **point vowels**, since they are visualised as three points on a triangle.

dissimilation The opposite of **assimilation**. A **process** whereby two adjacent sounds become less similar. For instance, in the history of Greek, a sequence of two **fricatives** in an **onset** was permitted in Ancient Greek, but these tended to become, over time, a sequence of a fricative followed by a **stop**, as in Ancient Greek [fθinos] ('cheap') becoming [ftinos] in Modern Greek.

distinctive features see **features**

distribution see **Phonemic Principle**

distributionalism A term associated with **American Structuralism**, whose practitioners focused on establishing the **distribution** of linguistic units in order to come up with an analysis. In phonology, this meant examining the distribution of **segment** types in order to assign them to **phonemes**.

disyllabic A synonym for **bisyllabic**.

domain A stretch of phonological material within which, or across which, or at the edge of which, phonological **processes** apply. Examples of postulated domains are the **syllable**, the **foot** and the **phonological word**.

dominant/recessive harmony A form of **vowel harmony** in which a property of a vowel in some specific **affix** is spread throughout the **root** to which it attaches, as in Turkana, where the root /ɪmʊj/ has **RTR** vowels, but when the habitual suffix /eeni/ is added, its **ATR** value spreads throughout the root: [ak-imuj-eeni]. Such suffixes are said to be dominant. In such languages, there will be other suffixes which are not dominant, as in [a-ɪmʊj-ɪ], where the aspectual suffix undergoes ATR harmony. Such suffixes are said to be recessive.

dorsal A term used to describe sounds in which the **body of the tongue** (the dorsum) features. The term subsumes **velar** and **uvular** sounds. It is used as a **feature** in theories of **distinctive features**, and as a **node** in theories of **feature geometry**.

downdrift A phenomenon found in **tone languages** in which the **tones** become progressively lower as the **utterance** goes on, so that a word with a high tone which is uttered near the end of the utterance may have the same **pitch,** or even a lower pitch, than a word uttered with a low tone early in the utterance. In the Kwa language Igbo, the following sentence has a sequence of alternating high and low tones, marked here with the superscript **diacritics** ´ and `: ó nà áŋ wà únjàígwè ('He is trying to ride a bicycle'). The last high tone, on the first syllable of ígwè, is close in pitch level to the first low tone, on the word nà. Also known as **declination**.

downstep A phenomenon found in **tone languages,** whereby a high tone has been lowered because of the effect of a preceding low tone which is not phonetically realised. In the Kwa language Twi, in the phonetic sequence [mí bú] ('my stone'), the second high tone is lower than the first high tone. It has been downstepped by the underlying low tone in the **underlying representation** /mí ɔ̀bú/. The underlying vowel /ɔ̀/ is then **deleted,** so that the cause of the downstepping is not phonetically present in the **utterance**. Instances of downstepping may well derive historically from **processes** of **downdrift**.

drag chain see **vowel shift**

Dravidian A **language family**. The Dravidian languages are spoken in Southern India. They include Tamil, Malayalam, Toda, Telugu and Kannada. These languages do not belong to the **Indo-European** language family.

DRESS Raising The name for a phenomenon found in New Zealand English, in which words of the **lexical**

set DRESS are **raised** from the **low mid** [ɛ] position to the high [ɪ] position, so that words such as *desk* are pronounced [dɪsk]. DRESS Raising forms part of a **vowel shift** in New Zealand English. Words of the lexical set TRAP are raised from [æ] to low mid [ɛ], while words of the lexical set DRESS move into the space of the lexical set KIT, and words in the latter set have a vowel that is shifted back to the **high central unrounded** vowel [ɨ]. Thus the claim that *check-in desk* in New Zealand English sounds like *chicken disk*.

Durand, Jacques A contemporary French linguist who spent much of his career in Britain, before returning to his native France. Durand has worked extensively on machine translation, but is mostly known as a phonologist who has worked on a variety of languages, especially French phonology, including the phonology of Midi French (Southern French).

duration A term used to describe the amount of time taken to articulate a given **segment**. **Geminate** consonants are said to be articulated with greater duration than non-geminates. **Long** vowels are said to be articulated with greater duration than **short** vowels. The term is clearly relative, but the phonetic duration of segments is more or less measurable in milliseconds. The main problem associated with measuring duration is that it varies from speaker to speaker, depending on context and rate of speech. There are also problems in deciding where exactly a given segment starts when one examines a **spectrogram**. Some phonologists distinguish length as a property of phonological representations with the brute phonetic duration of a given segment uttered on a given occasion.

dyslexia A condition which may be present from birth or which may be acquired as the result of brain injury of the sort induced by a stroke. Dyslexia is a reading dysfunction. Two main subtypes are identified. In surface dyslexia, the ability to recognise whole written word forms is damaged, but the capacity of individuals to access their **graphophonemics** may remain intact. In cases of phonological dyslexia, the damage is the other way round: affected individuals can recognise whole written word forms, but cannot access their grapho-phonemic knowledge. These phenomena are important for phonologists, since they suggest that graphophonemic knowledge is **modular** in nature.

E

ease of articulation The tendency that human beings have to produce utterances in which articulatory effort is diminished. **Assimilations** of various sorts are examples; if one utters an /np/ sequence in English sequences such as /ɪn + pʊt/ (*input*) as [ɪmpʊt], one makes a saving in articulatory effort by keeping the lips closed in the production of the **nasal stop**. Ease of articulation stands in a relation of tension to the need to sustain **oppositions** which signal differences in meaning. See **avoidance of homophony** and **Martinet**.

ejectives see **airstream mechanisms**

E-language External language. In the view of Noam **Chomsky**, notions such as 'French', 'German' and 'Japanese' are sociopolitical notions which do not constitute the object of linguistic inquiry. Rather, the object of inquiry is said to be **I-language**. Chomsky also argues that languages defined as sets of sentences constitute E-language.

elements see **feature values**

elide When a speech sound is elided, it is not pronounced. When French-speakers (who have no /h/ **phoneme** in their native language) speak English, they often elide the [h] sounds in words such as *happy* and *hair*.

elision A **process** in which a **segment** is not pronounced. In many varieties of English, words such as [fæmɪli] (*family*) can be pronounced with an elided [ɪ]:[fæmli]. In English, it is usually unstressed vowels which are elided. Consonants too may be elided, as in [sɪksθs] (*sixths*), often pronounced [sɪks]. The process is often referred to as **deletion**. For the elision of [h] in English, as in **Cockney** [æpi] for *happy*, the informal term 'h-dropping' is often used.

emphatic consonants Consonants found in the Semitic languages which are **apical**, but which have a **secondary articulation**, often in the **pharynx**. The **pharyngealisation** can spread to other **segments** in a word containing an emphatic consonant. In Cairene Arabic, the word for 'friend' is [sˤaˤaˤħib], where the **diacritic** [ˤ] indicates pharyngealisation. In this case, the pharyngealisation spreads from the emphatic consonant [sˤ] to the following two vowels.

Empiricism A tradition in the history of philosophy in which human knowledge is said to emerge from the interaction of the mind with the mind-external world. Empiricism has traditionally denied the existence of innate **cognitive** content, such as innate concepts. An Empiricist account of phonology claims that phonological knowledge is internalised from the environment, via social interaction with other human beings. Empiricism is traditionally distinguished from **Rationalism**, also known as **Nativism**.

empty onset see **syllable**

enclitic see **clitic**

Encrevé, Pierre A French phonologist who is known for combining an investigation of **sociophonetic variation** in speakers of French with an **autosegmental** approach to **Liaison** in French.

enhancement The idea that a phonological contrast can be perceptually reinforced, heightened or enhanced by the addition of some extra articulatory gesture to one member or members of the sounds in contrast. If a **back** vowel contrasts with a **front** vowel, the contrast can be enhanced if the back vowel is **rounded** and the front vowel is **unrounded**.

environment see **phonemic Principle**

epenthesis The insertion of a **segment** in a sequence of segments. The inserted segment is said to be epenthetic. An example of an **epenthetic consonant** is the **Intrusive 'r'** of **non-rhotic** varieties of English, as in *law and order*: [lɔːɹənɔːdə]. An example of an **epenthetic vowel** is the epenthetic [ʌ] in Scottish pronunciations of words such as *umbrella*: [ʌmbʌɹɛɫʌ].

epenthetic consonant see **epenthesis**

epenthetic vowel see **epenthesis**

European Structuralism see **structuralist linguistics**

eurhythmic see **eurhythmy**

eurhythmy In many rhythmic systems, there is a tendency towards sequences of alternating stressed and unstressed **syllables,** with every alternate syllable being stressed. Such sequences exemplify eurhythmy. The Malay word [ˌsa.ka.ˌra.tul.'m ã.ũt] ('near to death') exemplifies this. It has a (secondary) stressed syllable, followed by an unstressed syllable, followed by another (secondary) stressed syllable, followed by an unstressed syllable, followed by a (primary) stressed syllable, followed by an unstressed syllable. Such a word is said to be eurhythmic.

Everett, Dan A linguist who works on South American Indian languages, particularly the language Piraha. Everett is a controversial figure since he claims, among other things, that **recursion** is not an absolute universal of human languages. Everett is known for his work in phonology, morphology and syntax.

exemplar theory An approach to the **mental lexicon** whose central claim is that words are stored in the mind with all of the phonetic detail perceived by the speaker/hearer, including all **redundant** material. The idea is that each time a speaker/hearer hears a word, a trace of it is stored in the mind with all of the phonetic detail included. Thus, words which are frequently heard will have a large number of traces, or exemplars, which will form a dense exemplar cloud in the mind. Words which are heard infrequently will have weaker representation in the mind. Exemplar theory assumes that the human mind has a vast capacity for storage, and subsequent recognition, of visual and acoustic images. Phonologists who adopt exemplar theory deny that **underlying representations** in the mind are stripped of all predictable information.

exponence see **realisation**

external sandhi see **sandhi**

extrametricality Segments or **syllables** are said to be extrametrical if they 'do not count' in the calculation of syllabic or **foot** structure. Supposedly extrametrical material occurs at the edges of phonological **constituents**. It has been argued that, if one discounts the final segment in English words, it is possible to simplify the statement of the **word stress** assignment algorithm. If the final segment in a verb such as *astonish* is extrametrical, then the final syllable ceases to be **heavy** and the **primary stress** will be assigned to the preceding syllable.

extrasyllabicity One or more **segments** are said to be extrasyllabic if they are not integrated into syllable structure. The **floating consonants** which participate in **Liaison** in French are often said to be extrasyllabic.

F

fake geminate see **geminate**

falling diphthong a **diphthong** in which the most prominent element is the first one, as in English [aʊ] (sometimes transcribed [aw]), where the **off-glide** [w] is less prominent than the [a]. The most prominent element is often referred to as the **head** of the diphthong.

feature geometry The study of the way different **features** group together. Many believe that the **major place of articulation** features **labial, coronal** and **dorsal** group together in this way, and that this grouping may be represented using a **tree diagram** in which those features are seen as **nodes** branching from an Oral Place node. Similarly, the features [ATR] and [RTR] are seen as grouping together under a Tongue Root node.

feature values Some phonologists who postulate that **segments** are bundles of **features** argue that features have a binary '+' or '−' value, as in [+round], a feature said to characterise speech sounds which have lip rounding. Speech sounds which are said to possess the negative feature value [−round] are characterised as lacking lip rounding. Some phonological theories, such as **Dependency Phonology**, seek to dispose of such binary-valued features, and replace them with **elements** which are said to be either present or absent, so that sounds with lip rounding have the element [labial], while sounds which lack lip rounding are characterised as not possessing that element. On this view, feature contrasts are **privative** in nature (see **Trubetzkoy**). It is an open question whether there is any profound conceptual distinction between presence vs absence of an element such as [labial] on the one hand, and presence of [+labial] vs presence of [−labial] on the other hand.

features Most phonologists agree that **segments** can be decomposed into features, such as [round], [high],

[low], [front] and [back], so that the [u] vowel, for instance, possesses, among others, the features [round], [high] and [back]. Similarly, the [k] consonant is said to possess, among others, the features [high], [back] and [voiceless]. When phonologists speak of **distinctive features**, they mean features which function to signal phonological contrasts, such as the contrast between **voiced** and **voiceless phonemes**. See also **cardinal vowels**.

final devoicing see **devoicing**

Firth, J. R. (1890–1960) A British linguist based at University College London, and then at the School of Oriental and African Studies in London. Firth was sceptical about the extent to which the speech signal can be segmented into individual speech sounds, and this led him to question the validity of the notion **phoneme**, which was supported by his contemporary Daniel **Jones**. He adopted a **polysystemic** approach to phonological analysis and postulated **prosodies**, which are parallel to the autosegments of **Autosegmental Phonology**. An example of a prosody is the **nasality** which one finds in the language Terena, in which words such as [ajo] ('his brother') become [ãjõ], which means 'my brother'. In cases such as this, nasality appears to be a purely **suprasegmental morpho-syntactic** property. Firth argued that phonological properties such as this often had as their domain, not single segments, but larger units such as the **syllable**, the **phonological word** and the **intonation group**. There is a strong element of **instrumentalism** in Firth's ideas, and thus anti-**mentalism**. Firth also appears to have adopted the thesis that phonological objects lack **intrinsic phonetic content**.

Firthian Phonology see **Firth**

flap A speech sound type in which an **active articulator** engages in a brief contact with a **passive articulator**. Several varieties of English have an **alveolar** flap, transcribed as [ɾ], which is rather like a **short** [d], or like an alveolar **trill**, but with only one tap of the **tip/blade of the tongue** against the passive articulator. During the production of [ɾ], as in Spanish *pero* ('but') or American English *witty*, the tongue tip/blade taps briefly against the **alveolar ridge**. Also known as a **tap**. Although the **IPA** takes taps and flaps to be the same thing, some phonologists insist on distinguishing them. On this latter view, flaps are said to be **retroflex**, while taps are not; taps are said to involve a movement up and down of the upper surface of the tip/blade of the tongue against the alveolar ridge, while flaps are said to involve a back-front movement of the underside of the tongue tip/blade.

Flapping A **process** in which, historically, a [t] sound or a [d] sound has come to be produced as a **flap** (also known as a **tap**). The words *patting* and *padding* in **General American** are typically produced with a tap: [pæɾɪŋ].

floating consonants Also known as **latent consonants,** these are usually **word-final** consonants which are not realised unless they can occupy the **onset** position in a following word which would otherwise have an **empty onset**. The **Linking 'r'** of **non-rhotic** varieties of English is sometimes analysed as a floating consonant. The claim is that there is a word-final /r/ in words such as *far* in such varieties, and that it is floating, or **extrasyllabic,** but that it may be linked to an empty onset in phrases such as *far away*. Similarly, the 'latent consonants' which participate in the phenomenon of **Liaison** in French are said to be floating consonants, such as the /z/ of *mes* in *mes amis* ('my friends'): [mezami]. These floating consonants fail to be realised if the following word begins with a consonant, as in *mes gants* ('my gloves'): [megã].

floating tones In the literature on **tone languages**, there are two senses in which the expression is used. In the first of these, floating tones are postulated to be present in **underlying representations**, but are said to be unattached to any **segmental** material in those representations. In the Central dialect of the Kwa language Igbo, there are two low tones in the underlying representations of the words /àgbà/ ('jaw') and /èŋwè/ ('monkey'). But the expression 'jaw of monkey' is realised phonetically as [àgbaáèŋwè], with a high tone on the second vowel of the first **element**. Phonologists have postulated an underlying high floating tone, meaning 'of', placed between the two words, which attaches to the preceding vowel in the word /àgbà/.

In the second sense of the expression, underlying tones are postulated which in this case are attached to underlying segmental material, but that material is deleted, leaving the tone floating and potentially available to be connected with some other segmental material. In the Nigerian language Margi, the underlying sequence /tlà + wá/ ('to cut in two') contains a low tone followed by a high tone. A **process** of vowel **deletion** deletes the first vowel, and the sequence is realised phonetically as [tlwǎ], with a rising tone. It is claimed that, while the [a] segment is deleted, its tone is not. Rather, it becomes a floating tone which then attaches to the remaining vowel to produce a rising tone, seen as a combination of the floating low tone and the underlying high tone in /wá/. Also known as **latent tones**.

focalisation A **process** in which some **element** in a linguistic expression is highlighted. This can be achieved syntactically, but it can also be achieved phonologically, usually using **intonation**. If one wishes to highlight the word *John* in the sentence *John went to the pub*, one can place the **tonic** on *John*. This places the focus on *John*.

foot see **rhythm**

foot-initial A phonological **process** is said to occur in foot-initial position if the **segment** it affects is located at the beginning of a **metrical foot**. In most varieties of English, **aspiration** is at its strongest in segments which are in foot-initial position, so that the /t/ in *tack* is more strongly aspirated than the /t/ in *witty*. The /t/ in *tack* is in foot-initial position, whereas the /t/ in *witty* is in **foot-internal** position.

foot-internal A phonological **process** is said to occur foot-internally if it applies to a **segment** which is located within a **metrical foot**. **Flapping** in American English operates foot-internally; the /t/ in *witty* undergoes Flapping because it is located within a metrical foot, but the /t/ in *attack* does not undergo Flapping since it is in **foot-initial** position.

formalism Any conception of human language in general, or phonology in particular, in which human language is not seen to be **functionalist** in nature (designed for the function of communication), but is taken to be a formal object, in the sense of having **abstract** formal properties such as **infinitude** and **recursion**. The work of Noam **Chomsky** is formalist (anti-functionalist) in the sense that he denies that human language is designed for communication (instead, it is, for him, designed for thinking).

The term is also used to denote any set of formal devices for the representation of linguistic structure, such as the formalisms known as metrical grids used in **Metrical Phonology**.

Some linguists take the term to denote a way of describing human languages in terms of mathematical or logical formalisms. Some have argued that Chomsky's work is not properly formalist, in the sense that it is not properly mathematical in nature.

formant The cavities above the **larynx**, such as the **pharynx** and the **oral cavity**, act as amplifiers of the sounds created by the vibration of the **vocal cords**. Since all resonators have natural frequencies at which they will resonate, these cavities will resonate some frequencies, but not others. These resonances are called formants.

fortis see **lenis**. See also **fortition** and **aspiration**

fortition The opposite of **lenition**. A **process** whereby a **segment** becomes 'stronger', or more consonantal, moving up the **sonority hierarchy**. In the historical change known as Grimm's Law, the **voiced stops** of Proto-Indo-European (PIE) became **voiceless** stops, as in the case of the PIE root *gews* ('choose'), which became *kiusan* in Gothic. Processes of **assimilation** can induce fortition. Lumasaaba **morphemes** such as /li/ ('a root'), with an initial /l/, are realised with a [d] when a **nasal stop** precedes the /l/, as in the form [zindi] ('roots'). Here, the **complete closure** of the nasal stop carries over on to the following sound, changing it from an **approximant** to a stop, which is said to be 'stronger' (more fortis) than a **lateral** approximant.

frame theory of syllable structure A theory of how **syllables** emerge in child speech, proposed by Peter **MacNeilage** and his colleague Barbara Davis. The idea is that the consonant-vowel syllables found at the **babbling** stage of child development emerge from the rhythmic alternation of open and closed jaw, which in turn is said to have evolved from cyclic behaviour such as chewing in early primates. The open/closed jaw movement is said to provide the frame for such syllables, with the tongue and lips being carried by the jaw movement. With the tongue body in the **neutral position**, a sequence such as [bɐ] is produced, with a central low vowel; with the tongue fronted, a sequence such as [ga] is produced, with a front low vowel; and with the tongue body retracted, a sequence such as [gɑ] is produced, with a low back vowel. As the child develops, the tongue and lips begin to function as independent articulators.

free syllable Synonym for an **open syllable**.

free vowel Used in the analysis of English to refer to what are elsewhere known as the **tense**, or **long**, vowels in the vowel **phoneme** system of most varieties of English. The free vowel phonemes are all the vowel phonemes except the **checked vowels** /ʊ, ʌ, ɒ, ɪ, æ/. These latter vowels are also known as the **lax** vowels, or the **short** vowels of English.

frequency of occurrence The frequency with which a given word is uttered. Two main sorts are distinguished. **Token frequency** denotes the frequency with which tokens of a given word are uttered. The word *went* in English, which is an irregular past tense form, has a high token frequency; it is often uttered. **Type** frequency denotes the number of words belonging to a given type. Regular past tense verbs in English, such as *cried, shouted* and *kicked*, have high type frequency; the vast majority of English verbs have regular past tense forms. The distinction is central to **usage-based phonology** and the notion of **productivity**.

fricative see **degree of stricture**

front see **features**

front of the tongue That part of the tongue which lies below the **hard palate** when the tongue is at rest. It really ought to be called the middle of the tongue, since it excludes the **tip** and the **blade** of the tongue, which lie at the very front of the tongue.

frontness The property of being front (see **features**). Front vowels such as /i/ and /e/ have this property. Some phonologists, particularly those working with **privative features**, use the term 'palatality' as a synonym for frontness, to subsume both front vowels and consonant articulations made with the **front of the tongue**, the **tip** of the tongue and the **blade** of the tongue.

function word A term used to refer to words of a grammatical category. Important for phonologists, since function words are often unstressed in human languages, and often fail to receive the **tonic**.

functional category The same thing as **grammatical category**.

functional load The extent to which a **phonemic** contrast serves to sustain semantic contrast in a language, via **minimal pairs**. In English, the contrast between /ð/ and /θ/ is said to have a *low* functional load, since there are few minimal pairs based on that contrast, whereas the contrast between /p/ and /b/ is said to have a high functional load, since there are many minimal pairs which exhibit that contrast, such as *pat* vs *bat*, *pin* vs *bin*, etc.

functionalism Any view of language in general or phonology in particular, in which language in general, and phonology in particular, is taken to be driven by a major function: that of the need for human beings to communicate. Usually distinguished from **formalism**.

⎡G⎤

Gallo-Romance The language spoken in ancient Gaul after the disintegration of the Roman Empire and before the emergence of **Old French**, roughly from the end of the fifty century AD until the middle of the ninth century.

geminate A long, or double, sound, normally a consonant, as in Archi [lappus] ('to throw') or Finnish [poltta] ('burn'). The **constriction** in such consonants is held for longer than for single, non-geminate, consonants. Geminates are often represented as being connected to two **skeletal slots**, or two **moraic** positions, in syllable structure. When a long consonant of this sort occurs within a morpheme, it is known as a **true geminate**. When two identical **segments** happen to occur adjacently across a morpheme boundary, as in Archi [k'ossas] ('touch a knife'), they are referred to as a **fake geminate**.

gemination A **process** whereby a single, non-geminate, consonant undergoes lengthening to become a **geminate** consonant. For instance, in Malay, when a **root** ending in a single consonant combines with a suffix beginning with a vowel, the consonant undergoes gemination; thus the root /lətop/ + suffix /an/ is pronounced [lətoppan] ('explosion').

General American (GA) A term used to designate a range of American **accents** (known as **dialects** in the USA) which are broadly similar, and which differ from **RP**-type accents in several respects. Among these differences is **rhoticity** and the existence of **Flapping/ Tapping** in GA. GA is defined as not being a **Southern US accent**, and not belonging to the **non-rhotic** accents, such as the Boston accents, found in the northeastern seaboard of the USA.

generate A term used in **generative linguistics**. It has its origins in a branch of mathematics known as formal language theory, in which very explicit formal **rules** are said to generate, or characterise, or define certain sequences of symbols. In early work in generative linguistics, this aspect of formal language theory was applied to human languages. The term is often used to mean, simply, 'fully explicit', so that an analysis or an entire grammar is said to be generative if it is fully explicit. Some argue that much of generative linguistics has ceased to be fully explicit. The term was not intended to mean 'produce', as in 'produce electricity', but many linguists use it in exactly that way, talking of speakers generating **utterances**. The original idea was that a generative grammar, as an account of a speaker's **competence**, generated a set of **abstract** expressions, quite distinct from the utterances produced in **performance**.

generative linguistics Designates various different approaches, often associated with the work of Noam Chomsky, to the study of language in which the term **generate** is central.

generative phonology The phonological aspect of **generative linguistics,** associated with the work of Noam Chomsky. It is generally agreed that the founding book in this tradition is **SPE.** Generative phonology subsumes the SPE model, **Lexical Phonology, Autosegmental Phonology** and **Optimality Theory.** Some scholars see generative phonology as a continuation of **structuralist linguistics,** while others believe that the advent of generative phonology represented a radical break with structuralist linguistics.

Geordie see **Tyneside English**

gesture In certain models of the internal structure of **segments,** such as **feature geometry,** phonological **features** are bundled together into subunits within the segment. In **Dependency Phonology,** the two main subgroupings of features (**elements**) are the categorical gesture, which subsumes **laryngeal** features, and the articulatory gesture, which subsumes **place of articulation** in the **oral cavity.** In **Articulatory Phonology,** laryngeal and **supralaryngeal** gestures are said to overlap in the stream of speech and in phonological representations.

glide A name given to a class of sounds which are **vowel-** like, but which, unlike vowels, do not occupy the **head** position in the **nucleus** of a **syllable,** as in French [jauʁt] ('yoghurt'), [wat] ('watt'), where the [j] is a **palatal** glide and the [w] is a **labial-velar** glide. It is sometimes claimed that such **segments** can be considered as **high**

vowels occupying positions outside of the head of the syllable nucleus. In our French examples, the high vowels in question are /i/ and /u/, and the position in syllable structure is the **onset** position. Glides are sometimes known as **semiconsonants** or **semivowels**, since they are vowel-like, but often occupy syllabic positions in which one normally finds consonants. The non-head position in a **diphthong** is sometimes referred to as a glide, as in the French word [wa] ('goose'), which consists only of a nucleus, with [a] as the head of the nucleus, and [w] as glide within the nucleus, preceding the head. Glides of this sort are referred to as **on-glides**. Where a glide follows the head within a nucleus, it is referred to as an **off-glide**, as in the English word [aj] (*eye*).

glide formation A **process** in which a **nucleus** vowel ceases to occupy the nucleus of a **syllable**, and instead occupies the **onset** position of a syllable, as in French /lu/ + /e/ (the root 'rent' + infinitive suffix), which is pronounced as a single syllable: [lwe], with a **labial-velar** glide within the onset. Other examples from French are /ty/ + /e/ (the root 'kill' + infinitive suffix), pronounced as **monosyllabic** [tɥe], with a **rounded palatal** glide in the onset, and /li/ + /e/ (the root 'link' + infinitive suffix), pronounced as [lje], with an **unrounded** palatal glide in the onset. Glide formation is sometimes distinguished from **glide insertion**.

glide insertion A **process** whereby the vowel articulation in a **nucleus** carries over into an **empty onset** to form a **homorganic** glide. For instance, in Malay, /tari/ + /an/ (the **root** 'dance' and the suffix /an/) is pronounced [talijan]. Similarly, Malay /buru/ + /an/ (the root 'hunt' and the suffix /an/) is pronounced [buruwan].

glossematics see **Hjelmslev**

glottal An adjective used to describe sounds produced in the **glottis**.

glottal fricative A **fricative** made in the **glottis** by bringing the **vocal cords** together to produce friction. It is transcribed as [h]. An example can be found in the first sound in the English word *happy*.

glottal stop A **consonant** formed by **complete closure** of the **vocal cords**. It is transcribed as [ʔ]. Often, the **stop** closure will be released, as in the Scottish English pronunciation ['bʌʔəɹ] (*butter*). Because the closure of the vocal cords blocks the **airstream** and puts a sudden end to **voicing**, one often detects a glottal stop because one hears a very abrupt end to a preceding vowel.

Glottalic airstream mechanism see **airstream mechanisms**

glottalisation A **process** in which the closure in an **oral** articulation is accompanied by a **glottal stop** articulation. Glottalised stops are common in **Tyneside English,** spoken in the North-East of England. Examples are ['hæʔpi] (*happy*), ['wɪʔɾi] (*witty*) and ['pʰɪʔki] (*picky*).

glottalised Exhibiting **glottalisation**.

glottalling A **process** in which **oral stops** undergo **reduction** to a **glottal stop** articulation. Glottalling occurs in many varieties of English, as in **Cockney** ['wɪʔi] for *witty*.

glottis The space between the **vocal cords**.

Goldsmith, John An American phonologist known for his work on **Autosegmental Phonology**, Goldsmith is interesting since his training was in **generative phonology**, but he came to abandon that tradition in its entirety.

government A postulated relation between linguistic objects, often found in work on syntax. Transitive verbs such as *kick* are said by some syntacticians to govern their direct objects, as in *The man kicked the dog*, where the verb *kick* may be said to govern the direct object *the dog*. The term has been taken over into phonology within the framework known as **Government Phonology**, in which some syllabic positions are said to govern others. For instance, in the Standard French word *devenir*, the final **nucleus** position is said to govern the preceding one. The postulated government relations are said to give rise to the observed patterns of **alternation** in Standard French between **schwa** and **zero**, as seen in pronunciations such as **bisyllabic** [dəvniʁ] for *devenir*.

Government Phonology A framework within **generative phonology** which adopts an **element**-based approach to the internal structure of **segments**, and which sees segments as contracting **government** relations.

grammatical category see **lexical category**

grammatical word A word which is a member of a **grammatical category**.

Grammont, Maurice A late nineteenth-early twentieth-century French phonologist, based at Montpellier University. He is known as an early pioneer in studies of the way **schwa** works in French, notably **la loi des trois consonnes**. He also worked on bilingualism, in which he argued for the One Parent, One Language (OPOL) approach to bringing up bilingual children, whereby each parent sticks to only one language in addressing the child.

grapheme A unit in the spelling system of a language. Graphemes are usually distinguished from letters, since a given grapheme may contain more than one letter, but still act as a single unit in the spelling system. Graphemes which contain two letters are called digraphs. An example is the <th> grapheme used in English spelling, which corresponds to the **phonemes** /θ/ and /ð/.

graphophonemics The study of the relationship between spelling and pronunciation, more precisely the relationship between the **graphemes** of an alphabetic writing system and the **phonemes** of the language. A complete account of the graphophonemics of a language provides an exhaustive statement of all the grapheme-phoneme correspondences. See **dyslexia**.

Great Vowel Shift (GVS) A historical change which took place in the history of English. **Long vowels** shifted upwards in the **vowel space**, with vowels such as the **high mid** vowels [e:] and [o:] undergoing **raising** to [i:] and [u:] respectively, and the high vowels [i:] and [u:] undergoing **diphthongisation** to become [ai] and [au]. Present-day pronunciations of words such as *divine* ([dɪvain]) show the results of the vowel shift; they used to be pronounced with an [i:]: [divi:n]. In **Scots** and in certain **accents** of English, one can find words which have not undergone the GVS, such as the word *toon*

('town') in Scots, pronounced [tʰʉn]. In **RP**, this is pronounced as [tʰaʊn], since the historical [uː] diph-
thongised to [aʊ] during the GVS. The GVS has been
interpreted both as a **drag chain** (**pull chain**) and a **push
chain** (see **vowel shift**).

grounded see **grounding**

grounding A notion appealed to by some scholars who
postulate a clear distinction between **phonology** and
phonetics. The idea is that phonological knowledge,
by definition mentally real, is rooted in phonetic phenomena, where the term 'phonetic' covers facts about
the production and perception of human speech
sounds in social context. Many **processes** of **assimilation** are said to be phonetically grounded in the
tendency towards **ease of articulation**, as in the case
of assimilation for **place of articulation**, witnessed in
pronunciations such as [ɪmpʊt] (*input*), where the
nasal assimilates to the place of articulation of the
following **stop**. Those who argue for **phonetics-free
phonology** deny that phonology is grounded in
phonetics.

Guierre, Lionel (1921–2001) A French phonologist who
specialised in the phonology of English. Guierre elaborated an analysis of English **word stress** patterns
which departs from the Anglo-American **quantity sensitivity** approach. He also worked extensively on the
graphophonemics of English, claiming that English
spelling is, contrary to first impressions, a reliable
guide to pronunciation.

gutturals An informal cover term, not found in the chart
of the International Phonetic Association, for sounds

produced at the back of the mouth and in the throat, in the **uvular, pharyngeal** and **laryngeal places of artic-ulation**. There is some evidence that sounds produced in these areas constitute a **natural class**.

H

half-close Another term for **high mid**. See **cardinal vowels**.

half-open Another term for **low mid**. See **cardinal vowels**.

Halle, Morris An American phonologist who was profes-sor of phonology at **MIT** in Boston. He was co-author, with Noam **Chomsky**, of *The Sound Pattern of English* (**SPE**), and widely regarded as one of the founding fathers of **generative phonology**. Halle has worked on a wide range of phonological phenomena, notably **word stress** systems.

hard palate The front part of the palate, located in the roof of the mouth, behind the **alveolar ridge** and in front of the **velum**.

Hayes, Bruce An American phonologist who works in **generative phonology**. Hayes has worked on a wide range of phonological phenomena, including **metrical** structure. He is also associated with an interpretation of **Optimality Theory** in which **constraints** are said to be phonetically **grounded**.

head A term used variably in syntax, morphology and phonology. Several notions are appealed to in talking of heads. One is the idea of obligatoriness; the head of a unit is said to be obligatory. In phonology, one can argue that the obligatory **element** in a **syllable** is the

nucleus, and thus the nucleus is the head of the syllable. It can also be argued that a **metrical foot** must contain a stressed syllable, and that this is therefore the head of the foot. In phonology, the notion of prominence (**salience**) is also appealed to in talking of heads; the head of a phonological **constituent** is the most prominent element in that constituent. To return to our two examples: the nucleus of a syllable is said to be the most prominent element in the syllable and is thus the head of the syllable. Similarly, the stressed syllable in a metrical foot is the most prominent and is thus the head of the foot. Within **diphthongs**, it is often claimed that one **vowel quality** will be more prominent than the other, and is thus the head, as in the English **falling diphthong** [aʊ], where the [a] is more prominent than the **off-glide** [ʊ] and is thus the head of the diphthong. The notion head is often linked to the notion **dependent**; two or more elements in a phonological constituent are often said to contract a head-dependent, or governor-governee, relation. For instance, the head of a falling diphthong is said to govern the dependent, so that [a] governs [ʊ] in the diphthong [aʊ]. The head-dependent (or governor-governee) relation lies at the heart of **Dependency Phonology**, **Government Phonology** and **Head-Driven Phonology**. These theories apply the notion of head-dependent to the relation between the elements of individual **segments**.

Unfortunately, the term 'head' is used in some descriptions of **intonation groups** to mean something quite distinct from the notions just mentioned. In such descriptions, the 'head' in an intonation group consists of the first stressed syllable occurring before the **tonic** syllable, and any syllables following it, as in *John went to the pub*, in which the tonic falls on *pub*, and *John went to the* is said to be the head of the intonation group, since *John* is the first stressed syllable before the tonic. 'Heads' are not obligatory in intonation groups (*Go!* contains a tonic syllable, but no head); nor are they the most perceptually salient parts of an intonation group. This notion of head is thus quite unlike the notion described above.

Head-Driven Phonology An approach to phonological representation which takes the **head**-dependent relation to be central at all levels of analysis. Associated with the work of Dutch phonologist Harry **van der Hulst**.

heavy syllable see **syllable weight**

hiatus A sequence of two adjacent vowels across a syllable boundary, as in Standard French *le hibou* ('the owl'), which may be pronounced as [lə.i.bu]. Many languages exhibit hiatus avoidance **processes**, such as **glide formation** and vowel **apocope**.

hierarchical structure It is widely believed that human languages contain expressions, such as phrases and sentences, which do not consist simply of linear strings of words strung together like a string of beads. Rather, it is believed that those sequences can be subdivided into **constituents**, and that those constituents can in turn be analysed into smaller constituents. Thus, the sentence *I saw the man who shot the farmer* is said to be analysable into the subject noun phrase *I* followed by the predicate verb phrase *saw the man who shot the farmer*. This latter constituent can be said to contain the constituent *who shot the farmer*, which is said to contain the constituent *the farmer*. This constituent-within-constituent structure is hierarchical. Many phonologists believe that phonological structures are also hierarchical. For instance, **feet** are said to be analysable into their constituent **syllables**, which in turn are said to be analysable into their constituent **segments**.

high A term used in the description of vowels (see **cardinal vowels**). It is also used as a distinctive feature (see **features**), and to describe certain types of **tone**.

high mid Vowels which are high mid are articulated above the **neutral position of the tongue**, but are less **high** than high vowels. Examples are [e] and [o]. Also referred to as **half-close**.

historical phonology The study of the way the phonology of languages changes over time.

Hjelmslev, Louis (1899–1965) A Danish linguist who was associated with a school of linguistic thought known as **glossematics**. Hjelmslev was influenced by **logical positivism,** and attempted to devise a purely formal, non-**mentalistic** account of linguistic structure. The consequence of this purely **formalistic** approach is that his conception of phonology was **substance-free**. Hjelmslev also argued in favour of the principle of **structural analogy**.

Hockett, Charles (1916–2000) An American linguist who taught at Cornell University. He is often seen as the last of the great linguists associated with **American Structuralism**. Hockett remained critical of **generative linguistics** throughout his career; in 1968, he published a book which constituted a critique of some of the central claims made by Noam **Chomsky**.

homophone Two words are homophones if they have identical pronunciation. In many **accents** of the North of England, pairs such as *put* and *putt* are pronounced identically: [pʰʊt]. Homophones such as these constitute **minimal pairs** in accents of the South of England: [pʰʊt] vs [pʰʌt].

homophony The state of affairs whereby **homophones** exist. Phonemic **mergers** create homophony. See **avoidance of homophony**.

homorganic A term used to describe identical **place of articulation** of two adjacent **segments**, as in English [θɪŋk] (*think*), where the **nasal stop** and the following **oral stop** are homorganic (they are both **velar**) because the nasal stop exhibits **nasal assimilation**.

Hyman, Larry An American phonologist who works in the **generative phonology** tradition. Hyman works on African languages, and is known for his work on, among other things, **tone languages**.

hypercorrection A phenomenon connected with the attempt by a speaker to alter his or her pronunciation so as to approximate a pronunciation perceived as more 'correct'. Hypercorrection occurs when words which do not need to be 'corrected' are changed. Speakers with a native **accent** of English which lacks the /æ/ vs /ɑː/ distinction may 'correct' their pronunciation so as to say [dɑːns] (*dance*) when they attempt to speak with an RP accent. But they may also hypercorrect words such as *mass* to [mɑːs], when in fact it is pronounced [mæs] in **RP**.

hypocoristics Pet names or nicknames. These are of interest to phonologists, since they can reveal facts about phonological structures in specific languages. A simple example comes from French, where names such as *Florence* and *Didier* may be pronounced in their hypocoristic forms as [floflo] and [didi], in which the first syllable of the name is **reduplicated**.

hypocorrection A term associated with the work of John **Ohala**. The 'hypo' part comes from a word in Classical Greek meaning 'under'. Ohala argues that speakers sometimes fail to engage in **normalisation** (correction) when perceiving the speech signal. Take **velar** sounds, such as [k], uttered before a **high front** vowel; it is phonetically natural for there to be slight affrication of such sounds in that position. Often, this affrication will be factored out by the listener, who will hear words such as *kick* in such a way as to classify both consonants as instances of the **voiceless** velar **stop** [k]; the affrication is factored out as redundant 'noise' in the speech signal. When this factoring out fails to take place, the hearer identifies the **affricate** as an instance of an affricate, not a stop. This is hypocorrection: the hearer mistakenly assumes that the speaker he/she was listening to intended to utter an affricate, not a stop. The hearer can then, in turn, start to utter affricates deliberately in such positions. This, Ohala argues, is what lies behind the well-known sound change known as **Velar Softening (Palatalisation)**, which can be seen in historical changes such as that from [kɪkən] to [tʃɪkən] (*chicken*).

I

iamb see **rhythm**

iambic see **rhythm**

Iambic Reversal A term used to describe a phenomenon attested in English, in which prominence patterns are switched round (reversed) in phrases containing three **metrical feet**. In the name *East London*, the word *London* constitutes a **trochaic** foot which is more prominent than the metrical foot in *East*. But when *East London* occurs in the phrase *East London Airport*, the prominence levels of *East* and *London* are typically switched around, so that *Airport* is more prominent than *East*, which in turn is more prominent than *London*. Also known as the **rhythm rule**, since this is a rhythmic phenomenon.

I-language A notion found in work by Noam **Chomsky**. The 'I' stands for 'internal', since Chomsky believes that linguistic knowledge is mind-internal, rather than public. It also stands for 'individual', since Chomsky believes that linguistic knowledge is located within the minds of individuals, rather than distributed across social communities. Followers of Chomsky believe that a speaker's I-language contains a phonological component.

implementation see **realisation**

implicational universals see **universals**

implosive see **airstream mechanisms**

Indirect Syntax Hypothesis Unlike proponents of the **Direct Syntax Hypothesis,** proponents of this hypothesis argue that syntactic structure does not directly trigger phonological **processes**. Rather, the purely phonological domains which feature in the **prosodic hierarchy** are said to be the proper domains for the operation of phonological processes.

Indo-European A major **language family** which subsumes many of the world's present-day languages, including most of the languages of Europe and the languages of the North of the Indian subcontinent. The Indo-European language family was reconstructed in the nineteenth century, when systematic phonological and morphological correspondences were established between **Sanskrit**, a language of Ancient India, and Greek and Latin. Proto-Indo-European was spoken around the period from 2,500 to 2,000 BC.

inductive generalisations Generalisations which arise from the observation of specific instances. If a French-acquiring child often hears *Il a fini* ('He has finished') with the past tense of the verb *finir* ('to finish') and *Il est sorti* ('He's gone out') with the past tense of the verb *sortir*, it is possible for the child to form the inductive generalisation that the past participle of verbs ending in *-ir* is a form ending in [i]. Application of this generalisation, via a process of **analogy**, can lead to child utterances such as *Il a couri* ('He ran'), from the verb *courir* ('to run'). In this specific case, the form *couri* is an **over-generalisation**; the past participle of *courir* is the irregular form *couru*.

infinitude A property said by Noam **Chomsky** and others to be a formal characteristic of all human languages. If one assumes that all human languages exhibit **recursion**, then this guarantees that there is no limit to the set of well-formed expressions in a given language; the set is literally infinite. On these assumptions, it makes no sense to ask, for instance, how many English sentences there are; there exists an infinite number of such sentences.

insertion A way of talking about **epenthesis**. Phonologists sometimes argue that **epenthetic** sounds have been inserted into a sequence of **segments**, as in the case of the **Intrusive 'r'** in sequences such as *law and order* when pronounced as [lɔːɹənɔːdə].

instrumentalism A way of interpreting theories in which one takes theoretical constructs to be mere instruments for organising, classifying and making predictions about observable phenomena. An instrumentalist interpretation of atomic theory would interpret the theory as a mere device, without granting that atoms and atomic structure are real. Instrumentalism is opposed to **realism**. The **American Structuralists** are said to have adopted a purely instrumentalist interpretation of notions such as the **phoneme**.

interface A notion used by those who adopt any **modular** conception of linguistic knowledge. If one accepts, for instance, the idea that phonological and syntactic knowledge form separate modules in the mind, one needs to address the question of how the two modules interact. The point at which the two modules connect is said to constitute an interface. With respect to phonology and syntax, some claim that phonology does not interact directly with syntax, while others claim that it does; they have different conceptions of the phonology/syntax interface.

internal sandhi see **sandhi**

International Phonetic Alphabet (IPA) An alphabet designed to provide a symbol for every speech sound type which is capable of functioning in a phonological opposition in a human language. Provided by the

International Phonetic Association, the IPA is regularly updated in accordance with the latest thinking about phonetic and phonological categories. The IPA continues to incorporate the notion of the **cardinal vowels**.

interpretation see **realisation**

intervocalic Between **vowels**. **Consonants** often undergo certain **lenition processes** in this context, as in the case of the **voiced stop phonemes** in Spanish, which are realised as voiced **fricatives** or voiced **approximants** intervocalically, as in *la bodega*, pronounced [laβoðeɣɐ].

intervocalic voicing A **lenition process**, whereby **voiceless** sounds become **voiced** between vowels. For instance, the Korean root /pap/ ('cooked rice'), when followed by the suffix /i/, is pronounced [pabi].

intonation The kinds of **pitch** modulation which are found in whole **utterances**. Intonation contours can be used to highlight certain **elements** in an utterance, to bundle words together into information chunks, and to convey the speaker's attitude to what he/she is saying.

intonation group A single word, or a sequence of words, which forms an intonational unit, containing a **tonic syllable**. The written English sentence 'It's me, Tom' is ambiguous. If a speaker is addressing someone called Tom, then the whole **utterance** constitutes a single intonation group, with the tonic on 'me'. If the speaker is called Tom and is announcing that it's he who is there, there will be two intonation groups: 'It's me', with the tonic on 'me', and a second intonation group consisting of the word 'Tom', which constitutes a tonic syllable. Intonation groups are also known as

intonational phrases. One of the functions of intonation groups is to bundle up the stream of speech into information chunks. Also known as a **tone group** or a breath group.

intonational phrase Another term for an **intonation group**.

intrinsic phonetic content Among the phonologists who adhere to a distinction between **phonology** and **phonetics**, some believe that phonology is 'based on', or **grounded** in, phonetics. Thus, the rule of **final devoicing** in German may be said to be grounded in the natural tendency for **obstruents** to devoice in utterance-final position. **SPE phonology** incorporated the view that phonological **processes**, and phonological **features**, could be given a phonetic definition; they were said to have intrinsic phonetic content, so that a phonological feature such as [voice] could be defined in terms of the vibration of the **vocal cords**. Opponents of this notion argue for **substance-free** phonology; they argue that phonological objects are **abstract** in at least one sense of the term, and cannot be defined in terms of phonetics.

Intrusive 'r' see **non-rhotic**

IPA see **International Phonetic Alphabet**

isochronous see **stress-timed**

⊡ J

Jakobson, Roman (1896–1982) A Russian linguist who became an American citizen in the mid-twentieth century. Jakobson, a major figure in twentieth-century linguistics, arguably bridged the gap between **European Structuralism**, **American Structuralism** and **generative phonology**, since he spent the first half of his career in Europe and the second half in the USA, latterly at **MIT**, where Morris **Halle** was based. Jakobson co-founded the **Moscow School**, and later co-founded the **Prague School** with **Trubetzkoy**. Jakobson had a wide range of interests, including aphasia, poetry, phonology, Slavic folklore and child language acquisition. He adopted **Saussure**'s notion of the linguistic **sign**, and also a **functionalist** conception of the notion **phoneme**. Jakobson adhered to the concept of **markedness**, and attempted to state implicational **universals** based on markedness. He proposed that historical sound changes were **teleological** in nature. Jakobson also worked with Gunnar Fant and Morris Halle on an acoustic theory of **distinctive features** in phonology. His work on phonology also incorporated the idea of **redundancy**. Jakobson was a functionalist. He believed that linguistic structure was driven by what he took to be the main function of language: that of communication. In this respect, his views are quite distinct from those of the **formalist** linguist, Noam **Chomsky**. In the field of child acquisition of phonology, Jakobson argued that there was a major discontinuity between the **babbling** stage and the first words stage. This view was later discredited by Marilyn **Vihman** in her empirical work on infant speech.

Jones, Daniel (1881–1967) A British phonetician who worked at University College London. Unlike J. R. **Firth**, Jones argued for the validity of the notion **phoneme**. His conception of the phoneme was that of a 'family' (a set) of sounds. Jones is still known for his *English Pronouncing Dictionary*, first published in

1917 and still used by learners of English all over the world.

juncture A boundary or transition point in a phonological sequence. Junctures include **syllable, foot, morpheme** and **word boundaries.** Such boundaries are widely believed to play a role in certain phonological generalisations. In Scottish English, the morpheme boundary between the **root** and the past tense suffix in words such as *brewed* will induce **lengthening** of the preceding vowel. The lengthening does not occur in the word *brood* since there is no juncture between the vowel and the [d]; *brood* is **morphologically simple.** It is often said that some junctures are 'weaker' than others; the juncture between *could* and *n't* in the sentence *He couldn't* is said to be weaker than that between *could* and *go* in the sentence *He said he could go.* The juncture between *could* and *go* is said to be a full word boundary, whereas the juncture in *couldn't* is said to be weaker; *n't* is said to be joined to *could* as a result of a **process** of **cliticisation,** with *could* and *n't* forming a single **trochaic foot.** Weaker junctures are often referred to as **close junctures,** and stronger junctures are known as **open junctures.** In some cases, sequences of words which undergo such cliticisation end up undergoing **lexicalisation.** Examples are *cuppa* (from *cup of*) and *wannabe* (from *want to be*).

K

Karmiloff-Smith, Annette A child development expert and advocate of **constructivism,** who believes that she has found a middle way between **Empiricism** and **Rationalism.** She postulates innate biases in specific **cognitive** domains, such as vision, but she denies that there are richly specified innate **modules** of the sort postulated by Noam **Chomsky**. Her work has been influenced by Jean **Piaget** and is reasonably described as Neo-Piagetian. In the field of child phonological development, the work of Marilyn **Vihman** is broadly consistent with Karmiloff-Smith's ideas.

Kazan School A name given to two late nineteenth-century scholars and their students, based in Kazan in central Russia: notably the Polish linguists Mikołaj Kruszkewski and Jan **Baudouin de Courtnay**. Their work pre-dated that of **Saussure**. Like many Western linguists in later decades, they sought to develop what they took to count as a 'science' of language. In doing so, they attempted to find 'laws' governing the **synchronic** structure of human languages. They adopted the idea of the **phoneme**, and had a static theory of morpho-phonological **alternations**, in which statements about alternations are not taken to be statements about **processes**. It has been argued that their work influenced the thinking of Roman **Jakobson**.

Kenstowicz, Michael An American phonologist who has worked in **generative phonology** throughout his career, studying a wide range of different languages. He took over from Morris **Halle** when the latter retired as professor of phonology at **MIT**.

Kiparsky, Paul A phonologist known for his work in **historical phonology**, **metrics** and the phonology of English. He is the founder of the **generative phonology** framework known as **Lexical Phonology**. He played a prominent part in arguments against the **abstract** nature of the **underlying representations** postulated in **SPE phonology**.

$\boxed{\text{L}}$

La loi des trois consonnes A generalisation, postulated by the French phonologist Maurice **Grammont**, concerning **constraints** on **schwa deletion** in French. The generalisation states that a given schwa cannot be deleted if it would result in a sequence of three consonants. For example, in the phrase *Je te le redemande* ('I'm asking you this again'), the schwa vowels in *Je*, *te le*, *re-* and *de* may be **elided**, as in [ʃtələʁədmɑ̃d], where the schwas in *Je* and *de* have been elided, but not the schwas of *te*, *le* or *re-*. The phrase cannot be uttered as [ʃtləʁədmɑ̃d], since the elision of those schwas would result in the three-consonant sequence [ʃtl].

labial One of the **major places of articulation**. A sound is labial if one or both lips are involved in its production. Subsumes **labiodental** and **bilabial** sounds.

labial harmony see **vowel harmony**

labialisation A **process** in which a speech sound acquires **labial** articulation. In the North American Indian language Nootka, the initial consonant of the **root** /ki:ɬ/ ('making') undergoes labialisation when preceded by a labial vowel (a vowel with lip rounding), as in the word [ʔokʷi:ɬ] ('making it'). The diacritic 'ʷ' denotes the labialisation of the [k]. Labialisation is a form of **assimilation**; in this case, an otherwise non-labial consonant is 'picking up' labiality from an adjacent segment which is labial.

labiality The property of **labial** articulation. Labial consonants such as [p], [b], [f] and [v], as well as vowels with lip rounding, such as [u] and [o], are said to possess labiality. The property is represented as

[+labial] in theories of **distinctive features** which adopt **binary-valued features**. The **element**/feature [labial] is said to be a **privative feature** in element-based theories. Labiality enters into certain **vowel harmony** systems.

labiodental A **place of articulation** term which denotes sounds produced with the lower lip as the **active articulator** and the upper teeth as the **passive articulator**. Examples are the **voiceless** labiodental **fricative** [f] in the English word *fin*, and the **voiced** labiodental fricative in the English word *van*.

Laboratory Phonology (Lab Phon) The members of the Lab Phon community of scholars believe that laboratory techniques, such as acoustic analysis, are central to any properly scientific phonological investigation. Use of mathematical and statistical techniques is also central to Lab Phon. Prominent proponents include Janet **Pierrehumbert** and Robert D. **Ladd**.

Labov, William An American pioneer of modern urban **sociolinguistics**, Labov is famous for his work on **sociophonetic variation** in New York City and elsewhere in the USA, particularly his work on the sociolinguistic variables which underlie variable **rhoticity** amongst speakers of **New York City English**.

Ladd, Robert D. An American phonologist based at Edinburgh University who is widely known for his work on **intonation**. He is a member of the **Laboratory Phonology** community.

language family A group of languages which have a common historical origin. Examples are the **Indo-European** and the **Dravidian** language families. Much of the reconstruction of common historical origins has been based on phonological reconstruction.

language games It is common to find cases in which speakers of a language 'play around' with the pronunciation of certain words in the language, often producing a kind of secret language. An instance of this is the French language game known as **verlan,** pronounced [vɛʁlɑ̃], which is based on the expression *l'envers* ('the reverse'), pronounced [lɑ̃vɛʁ]. Phonologists believe that language games are based on systematic **processes,** which can reveal facts about the phonological structure of the language. In this case, one simply reverses the **syllables** of the word in question to produce the verlan version. In the case of phonetically **monosyllabic** words such as *femme* ('woman'), pronounced [fam], the verlan version is *meuf,* pronounced [mœf]. Some have argued that forms such as this provide evidence for an underlying **schwa** at the end of the word *femme,* which appears in the verlan form in its stressed form, [œ].

language-specific Specific to a particular language. The English **phonotactic constraint** according to which only /j, w, r, l/ may occur as the second consonant in an **onset** containing two consonants is a language-specific constraint. The term is not to be confused with the expression 'specifically linguistic', meaning specific to human language as a whole.

langue A term used by **Saussure** to denote a language as a set of **signs** which enter into a series of **oppositions.** Saussure claimed that langue, which he took to be social in nature, was to be distinguished from **parole,** which he took to be individual in nature.

laryngeal A **place of articulation**. Laryngeal sounds are produced in the **larynx**. The term is also used to refer to **laryngeal features**.

laryngeal features **Features** postulated to characterise **laryngeal** properties of speech sounds. Examples are [**spread glottis**] and [**stiff vocal folds**].

larynx The voicebox: a structure made of cartilage, located in the windpipe, containing the **vocal cords**.

Lass, Roger An American linguist who has spent his career in Britain and South Africa. Lass is a phonologist who specialises in the history of English, historical phonology in general, and the application of notions from the field of biology to language study. He was one of the first to query the explanatory power of the notion of **markedness**.

last lexical item In work on the **intonation** of English, it is often claimed that the basic rule for the placement of the **tonic** is on the last lexical item in a clause. Lexical items are words of a **lexical category**. These are typically nouns, verbs and adjectives. In the sentence *John went to the pub*, the most 'neutral' (**unmarked**) intonation would have the tonic on the word *pub*, which is the last lexical item in the sentence.

latent consonant see **floating consonant**

latent tones see **floating tones**

lateral Sounds produced with air escaping down one or both sides of the tongue are lateral sounds. An example is the [l] in the **RP** pronunciation of the word *lip*: [lɪp].

Lateral escape of air is distinguished from **central** escape of air.

lax The opposite of **tense**. Lax vowels are often said to be articulated in a more **central** manner than their tense counterparts, and with less **duration**.

laxing Any **process** in which a **tense** speech sound becomes lax. A well-known example is **Trisyllabic Laxing.**

learning by forgetting An expression used by the French psycholinguists Jacques Mehler and Emmanuel Dupoux. It is used to refer to a phenomenon attested in child acquisition of phonology whereby, in the first year of life, infants become desensitised to **allophonic** differences in the adult language. For instance, a child being exposed solely to **RP** will 'filter out' the purely allophonic distinction between **aspirated** and unaspirated **voiceless stops,** whereas a child being exposed solely to a language, such as Thai, where the aspirated/unaspirated distinction is **phonemic,** will not do this. The term 'forgetting' is something of a misnomer; the child is not engaged in forgetting anything, but is focusing on the phonemic contrasts in the adult language and classifying allophones as instances of 'the same thing'.

left-headed Used to refer to phonological **constituents** with the **head** on the left side of the constituent, as in the case of **trochaic** feet, where the head of the **foot** (the stressed syllable) is the leftmost syllable in the foot, as in the English word *happen*. See **right-headed** and **rhythm.**

length A term often used to describe the relative **duration** of a vowel or consonant. The **long** vs **short** distinction can be **phonemic** or **allophonic.** In the **Dravidian**

language Malayalam, [koʈːa], with a short [o], means 'basket', whereas [koːʈːa], with a long [oː], means 'castle'. Vowel length is phonemic in Malayalam. Similarly, [kaʈi], with a short [ʈ], means 'biting' in Malayalam, whereas [kaʈːi], with a long [ʈ], means 'thickness'. Consonant length is also phonemic in Malayalam. In Scottish English, certain vowels undergo **lengthening** before **voiced fricatives** or /ɹ/, as in [bɹʉːz] (*bruise*) and [bɹɪiːz] (*breeze*), as opposed to [bɹʉs] (*Bruce*) and [flis] (*fleece*), with short vowels. This is allophonic length. Some phonologists distinguish between length, as a **phonological** property, and duration, as a **phonetic** property. Long vowels in English are also known as **tense**, or **free**, vowels, and are distinguished from the **short** vowels, also known as **lax**, or **checked**, vowels.

lengthening A **process** in which a consonant or vowel is produced with greater **length** than it previously was. In the history of **Received Pronunciation**, the sequence /ɜɹ/ underwent lengthening of the vowel in **coda** position, as in the words *third* and *fir*, now pronounced with the long vowel [ɜː]. One kind of lengthening is **compensatory lengthening**.

lenis The opposite of **fortis**. Lenis consonants are said to be 'weaker' than fortis ones. The **voiced obstruents** of English are held to be lenis, whereas the **voiceless** sounds are said to be fortis. Lenis sounds are considered to be produced with less articulatory energy than fortis sounds, with greater muscular effort and greater breath force. See also **lenition**.

lenition The opposite of **fortition**. Any **process** whereby consonants become weaker, in the sense of becoming voiced and/or undergoing a diminution in **stricture**. **Intervocalic voicing** of **voiceless** sounds is an example of lenition. Anther example of lenition is the **reduction** of voiceless **fricatives** to [h], which happened in the history of many languages, such as Spanish, where the [f] of Latin *filium* became an [h] in *hijo*, which subsequently underwent **elision**. Lenition processes are often cited as evidence for the **sonority hierarchy**.

level-ordering see **Lexical Phonology**

lexical category Words of a lexical category, also called **content words**, typically include nouns, verbs, adjectives and adverbs. They convey substantial semantic content, and are often distinguished from words of a **grammatical** (or **functional**) **category**, which typically include articles, conjunctions, auxiliary verbs and pronouns. This is relevant for phonology, since words of a functional category often undergo various forms of reduction, are often unstressed, and often fail to contain the **tonic syllable**.

lexical-distributional differences A difference between two varieties of a language is said to be lexical-distributional if a given **phonemic opposition** is shared by the two varieties, but specific **lexical sets** in the two varieties contain different members of the opposition. In both **RP** and certain varieties of English spoken in the North of England, the opposition between **short** /æ/ and **long** /ɑː/ is present, so that pairs such as *ant* and *aunt* are **minimal pairs**: *ant* is pronounced [ænt] and *aunt* is pronounced [ɑːnt]. But in words of the lexical set BATH, North of England varieties select the short phoneme, with pronunciations of the sort [bæθ] for *bath*. The RP pronunciation of words like these is with the long phoneme: [bɑːθ]. This particular difference between RP and North of England accents often functions as a **shibboleth**. Differences of this sort are neither **realisational** nor **systemic**.

Lexical Phonology Also known as Lexical Morphology or Lexical Phonology and Morphology, Lexical Phonology is a model of the interaction of **phonology** and **morphology** which postulates different levels (also known as **strata**) of word formation, with different phonological **rules** and/or **constraints** holding at those different levels. Two levels of word formation have been postulated for English: one at which the so-called stratum 1 (level 1) **affixes** are added to **roots,** and a later level at which stratum 2 (level 2) affixes are added. It has been claimed that the level 2 affixes are more **productive** than the level 1 affixes. An example of a level 2 affix is the prefix *un-* in words like *unnatural*. An example of a level 1 affix is the prefix *in-* in words like *innumerable*. An example of a lexical rule applying at only one level is the rule of **degemination** in English, which yields forms such as [ɪnjuːməɹəbəl], with a non-geminate [n]. Degemination is said not to hold at level 2, so that words such as *unnatural* contain a (fake) geminate: [ʌnˈnætʃəɹəl]. This idea of word formation taking place at different levels is often referred to as **level-ordering**. The morphological and phonological **processes** in question are said to take place in a specific order: level 1 processes first, level 2 processes later.

Lexical Phonology also postulates a distinction between **word phonology** and phrase phonology, claiming that word-level phonological operations have distinct characteristics from phrase-level operations. In English, word-level phonology contains the kinds of affixation and process which we have just seen. The phrase-level phonology contains phenomena such the **Linking 'r'** of many **non-rhotic accents** of English, whereby a **word-final** underlying /r/ is said to be realised if the following word has an **empty onset**, as in *far away*, pronounced [fɑːɹəweɪ].

Versions of Lexical Phonology which contain **Optimality Theory** constraints (rather than rules) are sometimes referred to as 'Stratal Optimality Theory'.

lexical sets Phonologists, particularly British phonologists, who work on the pronunciation of different varieties of English, often appeal to a list of word sets proposed by J. C. **Wells**. These sets were devised to bring out the kinds of **accent** differences which exist between different varieties of English. Examples are the lexical sets THOUGHT, FORCE and NORTH. Words in these sets all have the long /ɔː/ **phoneme** in **Received Pronunciation (RP)**. Another example is the lexical set LOT, which has the **short** /ɒ/ phoneme in RP. The usefulness of these sets can be seen in the descriptive statement that, in certain varieties of English, such as **Standard Scottish English (SSE)**, there is a **systemic difference** with respect to RP: pairs such as *horse/hoarse* are **homophones** in RP, but **minimal pairs** in SSE. In RP, both words have [ɔː], whereas, in SSE, *horse* has /ɔ/, but *hoarse* has /o/. This /ɔ/ vs /o/ **opposition** has undergone a phonemic **merger** in RP, but not in SSE.

lexical word A word which is a member of a **lexical category**.

lexicalisation A **process** in which a sequence of words becomes a single word, as in the expression *wannabe* (from *want to be*), which can now be found in dictionaries, listed as a single word.

Liaison A **syllabification** phenomenon found in French. Many **word-final coda** consonants were **elided** in the history of French, as in words such *capot*, pronounced [kapo]. But some word-final consonants in certain words have remained as **floating consonants**, and will be realised, under certain conditions, if the word in question is followed by a word with an **empty onset**, as in *les amis* ('the friends'), pronounced [lezami]. Where the following word does not have an empty onset, the floating consonant is not pronounced, as in *les gants* ('the gloves'), pronounced [legã].

light syllable see **syllable weight**

lingua franca A language used by speakers who do not share a common language. Swahili is used this way in parts of East Africa. English often acts as a lingua franca among speakers of different Indian languages.

Linking 'r' see **non-rhotic**

liquid A kind of **consonant** in which one part of the **oral cavity** is blocked while airflow escapes through another part of the cavity. Examples are 'l sounds', as in the **lateral** [l] in **RP** *light*, and certain 'r sounds', such as the [ɹ] in RP *run*.

loanword A word from one language which is introduced into another, such as the English words *weekend* and *parking*, which have been borrowed by French speakers. Typically, loanwords are pronounced by speakers of the borrowing language according to the phonology of their native language. In our example *parking*, for instance, French speakers place the **stress** on the final syllable of the word, in accordance with the French **word stress** placement pattern. They also pronounce the <p>, the <a>, the <r>, the <k> and the <I>in a French way: [peʁˈkiŋ], with no **aspiration** on the **voiceless stops**, a French **central** [ɐ], a **uvular** 'r', and [i] instead of [ɪ], as opposed to RP [ˈpʰɑːkɪŋ].

loanword adaptation The **process** whereby **loanwords** are adapted by speakers of the borrowing language. Very often, loanwords are forced into the **phonotactic** patterns of the speaker's native language, as in the Japanese utterance of the English word *screw*: [sɯkɯɾɯ], which has three syllables, since **onset** sequences such as /skr/ do not conform to the phonotactic **constraints** of Japanese.

logical positivism A philosophy of science which is said to have influenced **American Structuralism** and thus the kind of phonological investigation practised by the American Structuralists. Working in the 1920s and 1930s, the logical positivists known as the Vienna Circle argued that truly scientific statements were based on observation statements. On this view, postulated unobservable realities had no part to play in scientific theorising. Applied to linguistics, and to phonology in particular, this led to an anti-**mentalistic** stance. Some of the philosophers who were members of the Vienna Circle were also members of the Linguistic Circle of Prague. See **Prague School**.

Lombard effect A phenomenon documented by Etienne Lombard in the early twentieth century, in which speakers are said to raise the volume of their speech to compensate for increased background noise. You can observe this if you go into a public space, such as a bar, early in the evening, and listen to the rising volume of speakers' voices as the bar gets busier. The phenomenon need not indicate a fully conscious decision to raise one's voice. A perception/production feedback loop is said to be involved in this phenomenon, and that loop is conceived of as central to speech perception and production. The effect is said by some to be interpretable as a purely self-orientated phenomenon (one wants to be heard), but is said to be an altruistic phenomenon by others (one is bearing one's listeners in mind).

London English A variety of English which has its origins in the working-class districts of the East End in the inner city in London.

long vowel/long consonant see **duration** and **length**

low Vowels which are low are articulated lower than low mid vowels, at the bottom of the **vowel space**. Examples are [a] and [ɑ]. The term is used as a **distinctive feature**. See **cardinal vowels**.

low mid Vowels which are low mid are articulated below the **neutral position of the tongue**, but are less **low** than low vowels. Examples are [ɛ] and [ɔ]. Also referred to as **half-open** vowels.

lowering Any **process** in which a speech sound is lowered, in articulatory terms. Normally used to refer to vowels which shift down the **vowel space**, as in the case of the lowering of the **high mid** vowel /e/ to **low mid** [ɛ] in French **alternations** such as *cafeteria*, pronounced [kafeterja], which, in its shortened, informal form, is pronounced [kafɛt]. In this particular case, the context which triggers the lowering is the **closed syllable** created when the word is shortened; the [t] in [kafɛt] is in **coda** position, whereas the [t] in [kafeterja] is in **onset** position.

Lyman's Law A well-known phenomenon in the phonology of Japanese which relates to **Rendaku**. Lyman's Law states that Rendaku **voicing** is blocked if the second **element** of the compound contains a voiced **obstruent**. An often-cited example is the combination of [kami] ('god') and [kaze] ('wind'), which does not become [kamigaze], but remains as [kamikaze], because of the presence of the [z] in [kaze].

M

McCarthy, John An American linguist who works in the **generative phonology** tradition. He has worked extensively on **Optimality Theory** and is widely known for his work on a **prosodic** approach to morphology.

McGurk effect A form of perceptual illusion in speech perception, in which subjects are exposed to a video recording of a speaker uttering, say, [ba], [ba], [ba], but the audio track features the sequence [ga], [ga], [ga]. Viewers frequently report that they have perceived a sequence [da], [da], [da]. Based on an experiment carried out by McGurk and McDonald in the 1970s, the phenomenon is said by some to show that lipreading occurs spontaneously in humans and is not just a special form of behaviour adopted by the deaf.

MacNeilage, Peter A New Zealander based at the University of Texas at Austin, MacNeilage is known

for his theory of the evolution of speech and handed-
ness. He argues that the left-hand/right hemisphere of
the brain evolved for the purpose of predation, and
that the right-hand/left hemisphere evolved for the
control of bodily posture, leading to left hemisphere
specialisation for speech. With his colleague Barbara
Davis, he is also known for the **frame theory** of syllabic
utterances of infants during the **babbling** phase.

major place of articulation The **labial, coronal** and **dorsal**
places of articulation. See **minor place of articulation**.

manner of articulation A synonym for **degree of stricture**.

marginal contrast see **derived contrast**

mark see **opposition**

marked In the work of **Trubetzkoy**, a member of an **opposition** is said to be marked if it possesses a property
which enters into a **privative opposition**, so that the /m/
in the opposition /m/ vs /b/ is said to be marked. A
further sense of the term relates to the **frequency of
occurrence** of certain sounds, or classes of sound, in
the world's languages. For instance, the **fricative** /s/
occurs much more widely than the fricative /θ/, so that
/θ/ is said to be a more marked sound than /s/.
Similarly, the class of **front vowels** tend to be
unrounded; rounded front vowels occur in the world's
languages but are rarer, and are said to be marked with
respect to front unrounded vowels. **Markedness** has
also been said to be related to sequence of acquisition
in child development; some speech sounds, or classes
of speech sound, are said to be more difficult to acquire
than others and are thus acquired later than others. It

is often claimed that a child acquiring a language which has both /s/ and /θ/ will acquire the former (the less marked segment) earlier than the latter.

markedness A notion which appears in a variety of phonological theories, from **Prague School** phonology to **Optimality Theory**. The idea is that **marked** properties of phonological **segments** and **constituents** play an active role in phonological **processes**, the shape of phonological systems and their acquisition. For instance, the unmarked shape of syllables is the shape which contains an **onset** constituent (containing one or more onset **consonants**). A syllable with an **empty onset** is thus said to be marked in comparison with a syllable which contains a filled onset, so that the English word *eye* is marked, in this respect, in comparison with the English word *buy*. Syllables which contain one or more **coda** consonants are said to be marked with respect to syllables which lack coda consonants, since the most basic syllable structure is said to be the **CV syllable**, containing an onset consonant and no coda consonants. Syllables with complex (branching) onsets are said to be more marked than syllables which have single onset consonants, so that English /bɹaɪt/ (*bright*) is said to have a more marked onset than English /baɪt/ (*bite*). It is sometimes claimed that certain phonological processes are sensitive to the marked vs unmarked distinction. Some have questioned the explanatory value of the appeal to markedness.

Martinet, André (1908–99) A French linguist who worked within European Structuralism (see **structuralist linguistics**). He worked in Paris in the late 1930s, then at Columbia University from 1947 to 1955, and finally at the Sorbonne in Paris. He is known for his claim, later reiterated in **Optimality Theory**, that there was a tension in human languages between the need to sustain **oppositions** in the form of **minimal pairs**, and the tendency to **ease of articulation**, which leads naturally to **homophones**. See **avoidance of homophony**.

Maximal Onset Principle A principle which states that, where a given consonant could constitute a well-formed **coda** consonant in a word or equally a well-formed **onset**, as determined by the **phonotactic constraints** of the language, then it is syllabified as an onset. For example, in the English word *appraise*, the syllabification [əp.ɹeɪz] satisfies the phonotactic constraints of English, since a coda containing only a /p/ is legitimate (as in *cup*), and an onset containing only an /r/ is also legitimate (as in *run*). However, the branching onset /pr/ is also legitimate (as in *pray*), so that the syllabification [ə.pɹeɪz] is also legitimate. The principle states that, in cases such as this, it is the latter **syllabification** which holds, since it maximises the content of an onset.

melody A term used to identify properties of **segments**, as opposed to properties of **suprasegmental** phenomena. **Features**, or **elements**, such as [labial], found in labial sounds such as [b], [m] and [u], are said to be melodic features.

mental lexicon The idea that the mind contains a vast stock of stored mental representations of words, linked together in multiple ways. The mental lexicon is not conceived of as a list of the sort found in dictionaries, but as a network of interconnected representations which vary in the extent to which they resemble each other. When we select the wrong word from the mental lexicon, this is often because we have selected a word which is similar in some way(s) to the word we were searching for, as in the statement by George W. Bush that 'coal prevents an environmental challenge', in which Bush selected *prevents* instead of *presents*; the two words have the same number of **syllables,** the same stress pattern, and differ with respect to only one **segment.** They are therefore closely linked in the mental lexicon.

mentalism A given form of linguistics is mentalistic if its practitioners postulate mental realities as part of the object of inquiry. Edward **Sapir** is known for his mentalism: he argued for the psychological reality of **phonemes** in the mind of the speaker. Noam **Chomsky** is a mentalist, of a specific sort; he postulates an innate **module** of mind devoted solely to language. That postulated module is often referred to as **Universal Grammar,** or the Language Faculty.

merger A term used in the **phonemic** tradition to denote a historical **process** in which a phonemic distinction is conflated. An example is the traditional phonemic **opposition** between front [a] and back [ɑ] in Standard French, seen in **minimal pairs** such as *pattes* ('feet of an animal') and *pâtes* ('pasta'). While the distinction is still given in dictionaries and can be heard in the speech of older speakers, the phonemes have merged for many younger speakers, and pairs such as these are now **homophones.**

metaphony A kind of **assimilation process** involving **vowels,** in which one vowel assimilates to another despite the fact that they are not strictly adjacent to each other in the stream of speech. The two main kinds are **umlaut** and **vowel harmony**.

metathesis A **process** in which **segments** within a word are switched around. In Lithuanian, **fricative** + stop clusters undergo metathesis when they occur before a consonant. The **morpheme** /dresk/ ('to bind') has the past tense form [dreske], with the addition of a suffix [e], whereas the infinitival form is [dreksti], with the addition of the suffix [ti] and metathesis of the /k/ and /s/. Metathesis also occurs in child speech, in utterances such as ['tʃɪkɪn] for *kitchen*.

metre see **rhythm**

metrical Relating to the **metre** (the **rhythm**) of a language.

Metrical Phonology A development in **generative phonology** which emerged in the early 1980s. Work in Metrical Phonology was chiefly concerned with **suprasegmental** phenomena such as **word stress** and **rhythm**. Metrical phonologists represented such phenomena using either grid-like visual representations or metrical trees. An example of a metrical grid follows:

```
          *
    *     *
    *  *  *    *
    *  *  *  *  *
```

Dundee marmalade

The idea is to represent the different degrees of **salience** of each **syllable** in the phrase: the more asterisks, the more salient the syllable. Here, the least salient syllable is the **penultimate** syllable in the word *marmalade*, which is unstressed. The most prominent syllable is the **antepenultimate** syllable in *marmalade*. The second most prominent syllable is the penultimate syllable in *Dundee*. The representation depicts the result of the application of **Iambic Reversal**.

metrics The study of the **metre** (the **rhythm**) of languages.

mid A **vowel** is a mid vowel if the height of the tongue falls between **high** and **low**.

minimal pair see **Phonemic Principle**

minimal word The minimal amount of phonological material required to form a word. If we analyse English **long (free) vowels** as VV (vowel-vowel) sequences, and English **short (checked) vowels** as containing a single V slot, then the minimal word for most varieties of English is (C)VV or (C)VC; there are no words consisting of (C)V. So word shapes such as [næ], [nʊ], [nɪ], [nɒ], [nʌ] fail the minimal word requirement for English.

minor place of articulation A sub-division within the **major place of articulation** categories, such as the distinction, within **coronals**, between **dental** and **alveolar**, or between alveolar and **postalveolar/palato-alveolar**.

MIT Massachusetts Institute of Technology. A prestigious East Coast American university in Boston. The birthplace of **SPE phonology**, since both Noam **Chomsky** and Morris **Halle** were based there.

modular Relating to a specific mental **module**.

modularity see **module**

module A term used in linguistics and **cognitive science** to refer to a specific component of mind which is said to be dedicated to a specific cognitive function. Relevant for phonology, since there are phonologists who subscribe to the thesis that the mind contains a language module. Of those who adopt this view, some believe that the putative module is innate (present at birth), a view associated with the linguist Noam **Chomsky**. Some linguists who subscribe to the idea of a language module in the mind (whether innate or not) believe that there is a submodule devoted to phonology. Others reject this modular conception of the nature of phonological organisation in the mind.

monomoraic see **mora**

monophthong A **vowel** in which the quality remains more or less constant during its production.

monophthongisation A **process** in which a **diphthong** becomes a **monophthong**. In some varieties of Yorkshire English and some accents of English spoken in the South of the USA, the diphthong /aɪ/ loses its **off-glide**, so that *cry* is pronounced [kɹaː], with a monophthong. Known informally as smoothing.

monostratal Involving only one level of **representation**. While classical **SPE phonology** postulated two levels of phonological representation (**underlying representation** and **surface representation** (see **surface form**)), monostratal models of phonology, such as **declarative phonology**, abandon this two-level, bistratal, approach.

monosyllabic containing one **syllable**. The English words **man, dog** and **cat** are all monosyllabic.

mora A term which is often used to describe the **length** of **segments**. **Long vowels** are often said to have two moras (or morae), whereas **short vowels** are said to have only one. Segments which have two moras are said to be **bimoraic**, whereas segments with one mora are said to be **monomoraic**. Similarly, **geminate consonants** are often said to have two moras, as opposed to short consonants.

moraic Relating to **moras**.

Moraic Phonology Any theory of phonological structure in which the **mora** is postulated as a significant phonological unit.

morpheme see **morphology**

morpheme boundary The boundary between two **morphemes**, indicated using a '+' symbol, as in /kæt + s/ (*cats*). Morpheme boundaries can play a role in phonological **processes**. In the case of the **Scottish Vowel Length Rule**, the presence of a morpheme boundary triggers lengthening of a preceding /i/, /u/ or /ʌi/, as in the word [əgɹiːd] (*agreed*), which consists of the **root** morpheme *agree* and the past tense suffix: /əgi: + d/.

morphological Relating to **morphology**.

morphologically complex Containing more than one **morpheme**. The singular noun *cat* is **morphologically simple**, whereas the plural noun *cats* is morphologically complex; it contains the **root** morpheme /kæt/ and the plural suffix.

morphologically simple Containing only one **morpheme**. See **morphologically complex**.

morphology The study of the internal structure of words. More specifically, morphology deals with units within the word which have an identifiable meaning or grammatical function. These are often referred to as **morphemes**. In the English word *unhappiness*, the prefix *un-*, the **root** *happy* and the suffix *-ness* are morphemes. Words such as this are therefore said to be **morphologically complex**; they contain more than one morpheme. Morphology and **phonology** are connected because of the existence of **morpho-phonological processes**.

morpho-phonological Involving the interaction between **morphology** and **phonology**. In Malay, when a **root** ending in a single **consonant** undergoes the morphological **process** of suffixation with a vowel-initial suffix, the root consonant undergoes the phonological process of **gemination**. Thus the root /lətop/ plus suffix /an/ is pronounced [lətoppan] ('explosion'). This is an example of a morphological process triggering a phonological process; the phenomenon is thus said to be morpho-phonological.

morpho-phonology see **morpho-phonological**

morpho-syntactic see **morpho-syntax**

morpho-syntax The aspect of linguistic structure in which both syntax and **morphology** play a role. Morpho-syntactic properties include properties such as singular vs plural, or present vs past, as in the case of the singular form of the English noun *cat*, as opposed to the plural form *cats*. Morpho-syntax is connected to **phonology** in many cases. In this case, the phonetic form of the plural **morpheme** is determined by phonological factors. If the **root** ends in /s/, /z/, /ʃ/ or /ʒ /, the **realisation** of the plural morpheme will be [ɪz], as in *horses* ([hɔːsɪz]); otherwise, if the root ends in a voiced segment, the realisation of the plural morpheme will be [z], as in *dogs* ([dɒgz]); and if the root ends in a **voiceless segment**, the realisation of the plural morpheme will be [s], as in *cats* ([kæts]).

Moscow School Also known as the Moscow Circle, this was a group of Russian linguists working in the early twentieth century. Influenced by the work of **Baudouin de Courtenay** and **Saussure**, these scholars were interested in the linguistic analysis of literary objects, including poetry. Chief among them was Roman **Jakobson**, who was later involved with the **Prague School** and then **American Structuralism**.

Motor Theory of Speech Perception A controversial theory of speech perception, according to which we perceive speech sounds by internally synthesising the vocal tract shapes involved in the production of a given speech pattern, and then seek to match these on to the incoming speech signal.

multilateral opposition see **opposition**

N

narrow transcription see **broad transcription**

nasal assimilation The **process** whereby **nasal stops** assimilate to an adjacent **obstruent**, as in the case of the

English prefix /ɪn-/, realised as [ɪm] in *impossible*, [ɪn] in *indirect*, and [ɪŋ] in *incredible*. This phenomenon is an example of a phonetically motivated process; the speaker anticipates the **place of articulation** properties of the **oral stop**, and produces a nasal stop which is **homorganic** with the stop.

nasal cavity One of the three **resonance chambers**. It refers to the space within the nose through which air may flow during the production of **nasal stops** and **nasalised** sounds.

nasal harmony A **process** in which **nasality** spreads throughout all of, or part of, a word, rather in the way that certain vowel properties spread in the process of **vowel harmony**. In Malay, nasality will spread from a **nasal stop** on to all following vowels and **approximants**, unless blocked by a consonant with **oral cavity** constriction, as in Malay [māh̃āl], where the [h] and the vowels undergo nasal harmony, but the [l] blocks the spread of nasality.

nasal spread see **nasalisation**

nasal stop A **stop consonant** in which there is complete closure in the **oral cavity** but **velic opening**, allowing air to flow out through the **nasal cavity**. Nasal stops are usually **voiced**, resulting in a kind of **resonance** which is readily identifiable as being nasal in character.

nasalisation An **assimilation process** in which a vowel becomes **nasalised** when it is adjacent to a nasal sound, often a **nasal stop**. In many **accents** of American English, the vowel /æ/ is nasalised when followed by a nasal stop, as in [pæ̃n] (*pan*). In Malay, a vowel *preceded by* a nasal stop becomes nasalised, as in [mãsaʔ] ('cook'). When nasality spreads beyond **segments** which are strictly adjacent to a nasal stop, this is often referred to as **nasal spread**, as in Malay [mãh̃ãl] ('expensive').

nasalised Involving escape of air through the **nasal cavity**. Vowels which are nasalised are transcribed with a superscript **diacritic**, as in the French nasalised vowel [ã], found in words such as *banc*.

nasality The presence of nasal airflow in speech sounds, namely **nasal stops** and **nasalised vowels**. Nasality seems to be able to function at the **segmental** level and at the **suprasegmental** level. In English, nasality is a property of segments, as in the word *map*. In other languages, nasality is overlaid on a sequence of oral vowels to signal a **morpho-syntactic** property, as in the case of the language Terena, in which words such as [ajo] ('his brother') become [ãjõ], which means 'my brother'. In cases such as this, nasality appears to be a purely suprasegmental morpho-syntactic property. Some phonologists regard [nasality] as a **privative feature**.

Nativism see **Rationalism**

natural class The idea that speech sounds fall into classes, or 'families'. Two main classes are **consonants** and **vowels**. Other subclasses are **obstruents** vs **sonorants**, and **stops** vs **fricatives**. It is often claimed that many phonological **processes** affect all of the members of a given natural class. For instance, **spirantisation** will often affect the entire set of **voiceless** stops in a language, yielding [f], [θ] and [x] instead of [p], [t] and [k].

Natural Generative Phonology A development in the history of **generative phonology** initiated by the phonologist Joan **Bybee**. This approach to phonological generalisations was founded on a rejection of overly **abstract underlying representations** which are at a considerable remove from **surface forms**. In the place of such abstract analyses, it was postulated that true phonological generalisations express **phonetically motivated allophonic** variation, such as **nasal assimilation**. For morphologically related pairs such as *divine/divinity*, Bybee rejected the **SPE** analysis, which involved postulating a single abstract underlying representation from which the **alternants** [dıvaın] and [dıvınıti] could be derived. Instead, she proposed that speakers store the alternants in their surface phonetic form.

Natural Phonology An approach to phonological phenomena which was a reaction to the **abstractness** of **SPE phonology**. In the theory bearing this name adopted by David Stampe, a set of natural phonological **processes** were postulated. By 'natural' is meant 'naturally occurring', given the nature of human perceptual capacities and the human speech apparatus. An example of a natural process is final **devoicing**, which is arguably **grounded** in the phonetic fact that the **vocal cords** will tend to cease to vibrate at the end of an utterance. Another example is the natural tendency for vowels to undergo **nasalisation** when followed by a **nasal stop**. It is common to assume that there is a **rule** of Final Devoicing in German, but not in most varieties of English. It is also assumed that there is a rule of Nasalisation in (Standard) French, but not in English. To account for the fact that these natural processes are not present as rules in English, Stampe argued that the child, in acquiring English, must suppress the natural process.

Another version of Natural Phonology has been proposed by Wolfgang Dressler.

Network English A synonym for **General American**.

neural nets A term used in the theory of computing to describe systems which are set up as vast networks of **nodes** which, when fed input, can apparently learn patterns in the input via a form of **inductive generalisation**. Neural nets are central to **Connectionism**, a theory of computation in which patterns can be identified by a neural net simply by the establishing of connections between nodes in the net, on exposure to specific kinds of input. The term 'neural' is used since it is suggested that such networks resemble the network of neurons in the human brain.

The emergence of work on neural nets in the late 1980s was important for linguists such as Geoffrey **Sampson**, who support **Empiricism**, since neural nets are said to start out as a blank slate with, it was claimed, no inherent structure. It has been argued that, if neural nets can learn linguistic patterns without initial built-in 'knowledge', then so can the brain of a child, unaided by the **Universal Grammar** postulated by **Chomsky** and his followers. Neural nets are important to phonologists who want to argue that statistical learning plays a role in phonological acquisition. See **stochastic phonology**.

neutral position of the tongue The position of the tongue when the **body of the tongue** is in the centre of the **vowel space**. When the lips are **unrounded**, the **vowel quality** produced with this position is **schwa**. The notion of the neutral position is central to the **cardinal vowel** system of vowel description, since vowels with the tongue raised above the neutral position are said to be **high,** while vowels with the body of the tongue lower than the neutral position are said to be **low.** Similarly, vowels with the body of the tongue in front of the neutral position are said to be **front,** and vowels with the body of the tongue retracted from the neutral position are said to be **back.**

neutral vowel A vowel which fails to undergo **vowel harmony** but none the less does not block the spread of harmony, as Hungarian [rɑdir-to:l] 'frog, ablative', where the suffix vowel harmonises with the **back** vowel in the **root,** 'skipping over' the neutral vowel [i]. These are also known as **transparent vowels,** since harmony 'passes through' them.

neutralisation A phonological contrast (see **Phonemic Principle**) is said to be neutralised in a specific context if the contrast is not attested in that context. For instance, there is a contrast between /t/ and /d/ in many varieties of American English, as in *tin* vs *din*. But the contrast is frequently neutralised **intervocalically** in **foot-internal** position, as in *bedding* and *betting,* both typically pronounced ['bɛrɪŋ]; the /t/ vs /d/ contrast is neutralised via a postulated **process** of **Flapping,** whereby either phoneme is realised as a **flap (tap)** in this context. See **absolute neutralisation.**

New York City English A variety of English spoken mostly by people of working-class origins in boroughs of New York City such as Brooklyn and the Bronx. Sometimes known as the Bronx accent, or the Brooklyn accent, this variety is socially stigmatised. Features include variable **rhoticity**, **raising** of the /æ/ vowel and **TH-Stopping**.

node A point in a **tree diagram**, such as the Place node in diagrams used in **feature geometry** intended to represent the internal structure of **segments**.

non-linear phonology A development in **generative phonology** which emerged in the 1970s. In the late 1960s and early 1970s, **SPE phonology** postulated phonological **representations** consisting of a linear sequence of **segments**, subsuming **features** representing properties such as **word stress** and **nasality**. Non-linear phonology involved the postulating of multiple layers of representation, particularly with respect to **suprasegmental** properties. The term subsumes **Autosegmental Phonology** and **Metrical Phonology**. The term is something of a misnomer, since all varieties of non-linear phonology incorporate linear sequences of segments or **syllables**.

non-rhotic A term used mostly in the study of English, but which is none the less applicable to other languages. A language, or a variety of a language, is said to be non-rhotic if its **'r' sounds** do not occur in the **rhyme** of a syllable. There are many non-rhotic varieties of English. One such is **RP**, in which an 'r' is pronounced in *run*, since the 'r' there occupies an **onset** position. In RP, there is no 'r' pronounced in *farm* or in *far left*, since the 'r', were it to be pronounced there, would be in **coda** position. All non-rhotic varieties of English used to be **rhotic**; the 'r' has been **elided** during the history of the variety in question. Some phonologists define non-rhoticity in non-syllabic terms; they say that non-rhotic **accents** do not have non-**prevocalic** 'r'.

Non-rhotic varieties of English often exhibit the phenomenon known as **Linking 'r'**, where a **word-final** 'r' is pronounced when it occupies the otherwise **empty onset** of a following word, as in RP *far away*: [fɑːɹəweɪ]. This is an example of **resyllabification**, parallel to what one finds with **Liaison** in French. Connected with this is the phenomenon of **Intrusive 'r'**, where an 'r' is pronounced despite the fact that the word in question had no 'r' historically, as in *law and order*: [lɔːɹənɔːdə].

non-standard A variety of a language which has not come to be viewed socially as a **standard** variety. Examples are **New York City English**, Midi French and Andalucian Spanish.

normalisation A perceptual **process** in which variability in an acoustic signal is factored out. When we articulate speech sounds, there is inherent variability in how we do so. For instance, a given articulation of, say, the speech sound **type** [æ] in English will not be articulated in exactly the same way every time we utter it. Speakers are able to compensate for this variability, such that they can categorise the variants as instances (**tokens**) of the same speech sound type. Normalisation is part and parcel of the process of the **categorisation** of speech sounds.

The normalisation process is not foolproof; we can fail to categorise a speech sound as an instance of the speech sound intended by the speaker one is listening to. This can, in turn, result in changes in pronunciation on the part of the speaker who has failed to normalise the speech sound. Some phonologists believe that this is the source of certain kinds of historical change in sound systems. In certain varieties of Spanish, the

Castillian (Standard Iberian Spanish) contrast between the **palatal lateral** /ʎ/, as in *calle* ('street'), and the palatal **approximant** /j/, as in *yo* ('I') has collapsed; a phonemic **merger** has taken place, in which both **phonemes** have come to be pronounced as the voiced **palato-alveolar affricate** [dʒ]. Thus, *calle* is pronounced [kadʒe] and *yo* is pronounced [dʒo]. It could be that failure to normalise affricated versions of these phonemes lies behind this merger.

Northern Cities Vowel Shift A **vowel shift** in American English which is said to have been under way for some time in the central and eastern cities of the North of the USA, such as Milwaukee, Chicago and Syracuse. The /æ/ **phoneme** in words of the **lexical set** TRAP is said to be **raised** to pronunciations such as [ɪ] or [ɪə]. The /ɪ/ phoneme in words of the lexical set KIT is **lowered** to [ɛ] or [ʌ]. The /ɛ/ phoneme of the lexical set DRESS is **retracted** to [ʌ] or lowered to [æ]. The /ʌ/ of the lexical set STRUT is retracted to [ɔ]. The /ɔ/ of the lexical set THOUGHT switches to [ɒ], and the /ɒ/ of the lexical set LOT is **fronted** to [æ].

nuclear syllable The **syllable** on which the **pitch** change occurs in an **intonation group,** as in the syllable 'pub' in the English sentence *John went to the pub.*

nucleus see **syllable** and **intonation**

O

Obligatory Contour Principle (OCP) A supposed 'principle' of phonological organisation, this is a statement of an observed tendency in some languages towards the avoidance of adjacent sequences of like elements. It has its origins in the frequently observed avoidance of sequences of like **tone** contours, such as HHL (High, High, Low), as opposed to sequences such as HLH (High, Low, High). The notion has been extended to other phenomena, such as the avoidance of sequences of **stressed syllables**. The idea probably has some foundation in a human perceptual tendency in favour of alternating opposites, such as sequences of **consonant** and **vowel**, sequences of stressed and **unstressed** vowels, or sequences of high and low tones. Whether it has any genuine explanatory power as a principle of phonological organisation is a moot point. There are countless examples of phenomena which violate this 'principle', because of the **phonologisation** of various phenomena.

obstruent The class of obstruents is a subclass of the class of **consonants**. Obstruents are characterised by a major constriction in the **oral cavity**, namely **complete closure** or **close approximation**. The term subsumes **oral stops, affricates and fricatives**. The other subclass of consonants is that of **sonorants**.

off-glide see **glide**

Ohala, John An American phonologist who has been a long-standing critic of **generative phonology**, which he takes to be non-explanatory and 'non-scientific'. Ohala seeks genuine 'scientific' explanations for phonological patterns, which he believes to be **grounded** in facts about human articulation, perception and social behaviour that, can be investigated in laboratory experiments. Proper explanation, for Ohala, is phonetic explanation. Ohala is known for stressing the role of the listener in phonological change.

Old English Used to refer to a period in the history of English stretching, roughly, from the seventh to the eleventh century.

Old French The language spoken in France from roughly the middle of the ninth century to the end of the fourteenth century.

on-glide see **glide**

onset see **syllable**

opacity An phonological **process** is said to be opaque if its original phonetic **grounding** is no longer apparent. Vowels tend to be longer before **voiced segments** for purely phonetic reasons, so that the **stressed** vowel in *bedding* will be somewhat longer than the stressed vowel in *betting*. When a given voiced/voiceless distinction is **neutralised**, the phonetic basis for such **length** distinctions may become obscured. This is the case with **Flapping** in American English; the /t/ vs /d/ contrast is neutralised **foot-internally**, so that *betting* and *bedding* are both realised with a **flap/tap**, transcribed as [ɾ]. The stressed vowel in *betting* remains shorter than the one in *bedding*, but the original phonetic motivation for this length difference has become obscured; the lengthening process has become opaque.

opaque vowel A vowel which fails to undergo **vowel harmony** and also blocks the spread of harmony, as in Tangale, which has **ATR** and non-**ATR** vowel sets, but where the low vowel [a] lacks a harmonic counterpart, so that [top-a] 'start' and [tɔp-a] 'answer' take the same form of the nominative suffix, despite the fact that 'start' is an ATR root, whereas 'answer' is a non-ATR root. When a further suffix is added after a suffix containing /-a/, it fails to undergo harmony, as in [ped-na-n-gɔ] 'united me', where the root /ped/ is an ATR root, but where the suffix /na/ blocks the spread of ATR harmony to the final suffix. Opaque vowels are also known as **blockers**; they induce **disharmony**.

open approximation see **degree of stricture**

open juncture see **juncture**

open syllable A synonym for **free syllable**. See **syllable**.

open syllable lengthening The opposite of closed syllable shortening. A **process** in which a vowel in an **open syllable** undergoes **lengthening**. In the transition from **Old English** to Middle English, the vowel in the first stressed syllable in a **bisyllabic** word underwent lengthening, as in Middle English *over*, with a long **mid** vowel, which comes from Old English *ofer*, with a **short** mid vowel.

opposition A term associated with the work of Ferdinand de **Saussure** and Nikolaj **Trubetzkoy**. A phonological opposition is a contrast (see **Phonemic Principle**), as in English /p/ vs /b/, exemplified by **minimal pairs** such as *staple* and *stable*. Trubetzkoy distinguished between different *kinds* of opposition. One type is the **bilateral opposition**. These are two-way oppositions of the sort /p/ vs /b/. Another type is the **multilateral opposition**, of the sort /p/ vs /t/ vs /k/, where the contrasts involve more than two members, contrasting for **major place of articulation**. Among the bilateral oppositions, Trubetzkoy identified **privative oppositions**, characterised by the presence vs absence of a phonological property, as in the case of **nasal stops** vs their equivalent non-nasal counterparts. Thus the opposition between /m/ and /b/ is a privative opposition; the former member contrasts with the latter in that it possesses the property of **nasality**. The property which may be present or absent was called the **mark**, and the member of the opposition which possesses this property was said to be **marked** for that property. The term 'opposition' is used loosely in literary theory to mean 'dichotomy', as in 'life' vs 'death'.

Optimality Theory (OT) An approach to the study of phonological phenomena which replaces the notion of **rule** with the notion **constraint**. In OT, constraints are said to be violable, so that a constraint banning **voiced obstruents** in **word-final** position would be violated in a language which permits voiced obstruents in that position. Constraints are also said to be capable of clashing with each other, i.e. coming into conflict. A constraint which is said by some to be universal (but violable) is the proposed constraint that the voicing state of a given **segment** must remain the same in its **surface form**. In a language which has **Word-Final Devoicing**, such as German, this universal constraint comes into conflict with the constraint which bans voiced obstruents in word-final position. In OT, constraints are said to be ranked differently in different languages. In our German case, the constraint banning voiced obstruents is said to 'outrank', or predominate over, the universal constraint. In a language which has voiced obstruents word-finally, the ranking is reversed.

   In some interpretations of OT, all constraints are said to be **universal**, given by **Universal Grammar**. Other interpretations reject this view and argue that all constraints are **language-specific**. There is debate as to whether constraints should be seen as phonetically **grounded** or not.

oral Sounds in which there is no airflow through the **nasal cavity** are called oral sounds. During the production of these sounds, there is **velic closure**. Examples are **oral stops**, such as [p] and [d], **fricatives** such as [f] and [s], and **affricates** such as [dz] and [tʃ].

oral cavity That part of the **vocal tract** above the **pharynx**, excluding the **nasal cavity**.

oral stop A **stop** consonant in which the **velum** (soft palate) is raised. This **velic closure** prevents nasal airflow. Examples of oral stops are [t] and [b].

over-generalisation A phenomenon attested in child language acquisition, in which children grasp a phonological, morphological or syntactic **rule** and apply it to forms it does not apply to in adult speech. Examples are child utterances such as *I catched the butterfly*, which suggest that the child has grasped the generalisation for forming regular past tense forms of English verbs, but has over-generalised it to irregular forms such as the past tense of the verb *catch*. Children pass through this phase and eventually master the irregular forms, especially if they are high in **frequency**.

oxytone A word which has **primary stress** on the final **syllable**, as in the English word *deny*.

| P |

palatal Sounds in which the **active articulator** is the **front of the tongue** and the **passive articulator** is the **hard**

palate are said to be palatal. An example is the palatal **approximant** [j] in the English word *yes*.

palatalisation A **process** in which non-**palatal** sounds become palatal or **postalveolar**. It is common for **velar** sounds to become palatalised before **front vowels**. The postalveolar **fricative** [ʃ] found in French words such as *cher* ('expensive') was a velar [k] in Latin which palatalised to become the postalveolar **affricate** [tʃ], and then became [ʃ]. Processes in which velars undergo fronting to become **alveolar** sounds are also sometimes referred to as palatalisation processes. The velar **stop** [k] in Latin was fronted to the alveolar affricate [ts] before the high front vowel [i] in **Gallo-Romance**, and later became [s] in **Old French**; the initial [s] in the modern French word *ciel* ('sky') was a [k] in Latin. In the description of English, palatalisation is referred to informally as **velar softening**, found in present-day **alternations** such as *electric*, ending with velar [k] and *electricity*, in which an [s] is found before the suffix *-ity*.

palatality see **frontness**

palato-alveolar see **postalveolar**

paradigm A term used both in **morphology** and in **phonology**. Although there is some variability in the way it is used, it often denotes a set of related word forms, such as the French pronouns *moi, toi, lui, elle, nous, vous, eux, elles*. These are said to stand in a **paradigmatic** relationship, in that each can be substituted for the other in a given structural slot, such as the structure *Il est chez____*, where use of *moi* yields *Il est chez moi* ('He's at my place'), whereas use of *toi* yields *Il est chez toi* ('He's at your place'). The term is also used for sets of morphologically related words, such as *kind*, *unkind*, *kindness*, *kindly*, *kindliness*, *unkindliness*, etc. See **paradigm uniformity** effect.

paradigm uniformity effect A phonological phenomenon in which the **paradigmatic** relatedness of words has an effect on phonological **processes**. In **General American**, the process of **Flapping** occurs **foot-internally**, so that it will occur in the word *city*, but not in the word *military*, which has two metrical **feet** in American English: ['mɪlɪ] [ˌteɹi], with **primary stress** on the ['mɪ] and **secondary stress** on the [ˌtɛ]. Because the /t/ in [ˌtɛ] is in **foot-initial** position, it cannot undergo Flapping. When one forms the paradigmatically related word *militaristic*, the primary stress shifts: [ˌmɪlɪtəɹ'ɪstɪk], with primary stress on the ['ɪs]. The /t/ in question is now in foot-internal position, so one would expect it to undergo Flapping, but it does not. Phonologists believe that, in cases like this, the morphological relatedness of the words in question acts to block the phonological process; in retaining the non-flapped pronunciation, one is retaining a degree of uniformity in the phonetic shape of the members of the **paradigm**.

paradigmatic Two items stand in a paradigmatic relation if they belong to the same **paradigm**.

Paradis, Carole A Canadian phonologist associated with the Theory of Constraints and Repair Strategies. See **constraint** and **repair strategies**.

parallel distribution see **Phonemic Principle**

parameter The term is sometimes used in a relatively non-technical way, in its ordinary everyday sense, to mean some feature according to which languages, or varieties of a language, vary, as in the example 'If we consider the parameter of lip rounding, we find that back vowels tend to be **rounded**, whereas front vowels tend not to be.' **Sociolinguistic** parameters are also appealed to in work on **sociophonetic variation**. For instance, the parameter of social class correlates with degree of **non-rhoticity** among speakers of **New York City English**: the lower the social class of a speaker, the more non-rhotic the speaker is likely to be.

Used in a more technical sense by those who adopt a **principles and parameters approach** to **generative linguistics**. Applied to **phonology**, postulated parameters include selecting **left-headed** vs **right-headed** foot structures.

parole A term used by **Saussure** to denote individual acts of uttering. Saussure distinguished parole and **langue**.

paroxytone A word which has **primary stress** on the **penultimate syllable**, as in the English word *city*.

passive articulator see **active articulator**

Peirce, C. S. (1839–1914) An American philosopher whose work has implications for linguistics in general, and phonology in particular. His conception of **signs** is distinct from Saussure's; for Peirce, a sign was a mind-external object, as opposed to a connection between an acoustic image and a concept. Peirce divided signs into three sorts: indices, icons and symbols. It is symbols which act as linguistic signs, for Peirce. The distinction between **type** and **token**, much used in linguistics, including phonology, stems from Peirce's work.

penultimate Second last. Often used to refer to the position of a **syllable** in a word for the purposes of **word stress** assignment.

performance A term associated with the work of Noam Chomsky, and thus much used in **generative linguistics**. It designates use of linguistic knowledge in a specific context of utterance, as distinct from linguistic knowledge per se (referred to as **competence**). Some linguists argue that the competence/performance distinction is untenable. Others wish to retain it, but to focus as much on performance as on competence. The competence/performance distinction bears some similarity to **Saussure**'s **langue/parole** distinction, but they differ in at least two major respects. Competence is located within the individual for Chomsky, and performance is located in social context. For Saussure, langue is social, not individual, while parole is individual. For Saussure, langue is an inventory of signs. For Chomsky, competence is not; it is a mind-internal grammar. See **I-language** and **E-language**.

pharyngeal Articulated in the **pharynx**.

pharyngealisation A kind of **secondary articulation** in which there is constriction in the **pharynx**. To transcribe such sounds using the **IPA**, a superscript **diacritic** [ˤ] is placed after the relevant symbol, as in the Arabic word [tˤiːn] ('mud').

pharynx One of the three **resonance chambers** in the **vocal tract**, stretching from the **larynx** up to the **oral cavity**.

phoneme The term dates at least as far back as the work of the nineteenth-century Polish linguist Jan **Baudouin**

de Courtnay. There is more than one definition of the phoneme in the phonological literature. It is common to find a phoneme defined as a kind of sound, a distinctive sound in a specific language. By 'distinctive' is meant 'having a **contrastive function**', where the contrast in question is semantic (related to meaning), as in the distinction between [lɪp] (*lip*) and [sɪp] (*sip*) in English; the substitution of one sound-type ([s]) for another ([l]) results in a change of word meaning. This view is a rather **concrete**, or phonetic, conception of the phoneme. A variant on this concrete view is that a phoneme is a set, or family, of distinct speech sound types which count as 'the same thing'. This variant version is more **abstract** than the idea that phonemes are literally sounds, since sets are not sounds; they are abstract, in some sense. Another view is more **mentalistic** than this. On one version of this view, phonemes are not sounds and cannot be heard, since they are mental categories. These first two views are based on **realism**. A third view takes phonemes to be no more than theoretical constructs, devised by the linguist as convenient fictions, in order to provide a picture of the sound patterns in a specific language. This view is based on **instrumentalism**. Some phonologists, such as **Trubetzkoy**, have argued for a functional view of phonemes; for Trubetzkoy, one must identify phonemes on the basis of their function in the phoneme system of a particular language. Trubetzkoy's view of phonemes seems to be neither phonetic, nor mentalistic, nor instrumentalist. All of these interpretations of the notion 'phoneme' assume the validity of the **Phonemic Principle**. Some linguists deny the existence of phonemes; they believe that the phoneme notion arises from the influence of alphabetic writing systems on phonologists' analyses. It is the norm to represent phonemes using **slanted brackets**, as in the case of the English word *pull*: /pʊl/. **Square brackets** are used in **phonetic transcriptions** which show allophonic detail: [pʰʊɫ].

phonemic see **phoneme**

Phonemic Principle Whatever view one takes of the existence, or the status, of **phonemes**, one finds a cluster of notions which constitute the Phonemic Principle. Central to this method is the idea of **distribution**. The distribution of a sound type, such as [l] in **RP**, is the range of **environments** in which it can occur. An environment is a specific structural slot in which a sound can occur, such as the **onset** of a syllable, or **word-initial** position, or **intervocalic** position. The sound [l] in RP has the following distribution: it occurs only in onsets, as in the word [lɪp] (*lip*). The sound [ɫ], often known as 'dark l', has a different distribution in RP: it occurs only in **rhymes**, as in [pʰiːɫ] (*peel*), where it occurs in **coda** position, and [kʰʌpɫ] (*couple*), where it occurs in **nucleus** position. When two or more sounds exhibit this kind of non-overlapping distribution, they are said to occur in **complementary distribution**. Once it is established that two or more sounds are in complementary distribution, we may ask whether the sounds in question are phonetically similar. In this case, they are; both are **laterals**, both are **voiced**, both have an **alveolar** articulation. Once we have established complementary distribution and phonetic similarity, we say that the two (or more) sounds are **allophones** of the same phoneme. Allophones are said to be **rule-governed**, predictable **realisations** of phonemes. In this case the rule is: the /l/ phoneme is realised as [l] in onsets, and as [ɫ] in rhymes. Two or more sounds are said to have overlapping, or

parallel, distribution, if there is at least one structural slot in which either sound can occur. This is true for the two sounds [l] and [s] in RP; both may occur in **word-initial** onsets before a stressed vowel, as in [lɪp] (*lip*) and [sɪp] (*sip*). Once we have established that two sounds are in parallel distribution, we may establish whether they have a **contrastive function**: that is, whether the presence of one rather than the other may signal a difference in meaning. This is the case here: [lɪp] does not mean the same thing as [sɪp]. Pairs of words of this sort are known as **minimal pairs**. A minimal pair is a pair of words which differ with respect to only one sound. Once we have established that two or more sounds have parallel distribution and that they function contrastively, we say that they are realisations of different phonemes, in this case /l/ and /s/.

Phonemic contrasts are often known as phonemic **oppositions**. Typically, the set of phonemic oppositions in a language is systematic; the oppositions form a phonemic system. In English, /p/ stands in opposition to /b/, and the same is true of /t/ vs /d/ and /k/ vs /g/. We have here a system of phonemic oppositions which is symmetrical; in each case, we find an opposition between a **voiceless** member and a voiced member. We therefore say that the phonetic property of **voicing** is **phonemic** for **stops** in English. This is different from the phonetic property of **velarisation** which we saw in RP [ɫ], as distinct from RP [l]. Since these two sounds are allophones of the phoneme /l/ in RP, we say that velarisation is **allophonic** in RP. A given phonetic property may be allophonic in one language but phonemic in another. For instance, voicing is allophonic for stops in Korean; there are no voiced stop phonemes in Korean, but Korean has voiced stop allophones of the phonemes /p/, /t/ and /k/.

Vowel phonemes are also typically organised into phonemic systems of opposition. For instance, French has a series of front **unrounded** vowel phonemes: /i/, /e/, /ɛ/. It also has a corresponding set of front **rounded** vowel phonemes: /y/, /ø/, /œ/. Once again, the system of oppositions is symmetrical. Not all sets of phonemic oppositions are symmetrical, but there is a general tendency towards symmetricality. An alternative to this picture of the way oppositions work is the **polysystemic** approach. It should be noted that some scholars argue that the idea of the phoneme is based solely on knowledge of alphabetic writing systems and that phonemes do not exist. Others argue that, to the contrary, when an alphabetic writing system is invented, it taps into intuitions based on pre-existing, mentally real phonemes.

phonemic transcription Strictly speaking, this ought to be a form of visual representation of a word, or sequence of words, which contains only symbols representing the **phonemes** of the language. A strictly phonemic transcription of the **RP** word *pull* ought to contain only three symbols for the three phonemes in the word: /pʊl/. Phonemic transcriptions ought not to show **allophones**. In our example, the difference between a phonemic transcription of the word and a phonetic transcription is that the **aspiration** on the /p/ and the **velarisation** of the /l/ would be represented in the phonetic transcription: [pʰʊɫ]. However, the reality in many pronouncing dictionaries is that supposedly phonemic transcriptions do indeed contain representations of allophones. An example of this is the representation in such dictionaries of the **tap** in **General American**; transcriptions such as /sɪɾi/ for the word *city* ought to be /sɪti/ if they are to be truly phonemic, since the tap is an allophone of the phonemes /t/ and /d/. It is clear what the practical advantage is of representing allophones such as taps, but in doing so, dictionary editors are providing transcriptions which are not strictly phonemic.

phonetic transcription see **phonemic transcription**

phonetically motivated A **process** is said to be phonetically motivated if it can be shown to be driven by facts about acoustics, articulation or the perception of speech sounds. An example of a phonetically motivated process is the phenomenon of **voicing assimilation** in **obstruents**, as in the case of Polish /gorod/ ('town'), which has a **voiceless stop** at the end of the **base** when the diminutive suffix /-ka/ is added: [gorotka] ('little town'). This is a form of anticipatory assimilation, in which the voicelessness of the [k] is anticipated, resulting in devoicing of the /d/ at the end of the base. Such assimilations are driven by facts about articulation.

phonetics The study of human speech sounds. Often subdivided into articulatory phonetics (the study of how human speech sounds are made) and acoustic phonetics (the study of the acoustic properties of those sounds). There is no universal consensus on the distinction and relation between phonetics and **phonology**. See **realisation**.

phonetics-free phonology Any conception of phonological objects in which they are said not to be definable in terms of **phonetics**. It appears that this view was adopted by the Danish linguist Louis **Hjelmslev** and the British linguist J. R. **Firth**. The idea recurs throughout the history of **phonology**, appearing in work on **Government Phonology** and in the notion of 'substance abuse', associated with the writings of Mark Hale and Charles Reiss. Here, 'substance' means 'phonetic substance', which they take to be misused if incorporated into our account of phonological, as opposed to phonetic, objects.

phonological phrase A **prosodic** unit postulated by some phonologists, often said to constitute one of the units in the **prosodic hierarchy**. In the analysis of the **process** of **Liaison** in French, it is possible to argue that a sequence of a determiner and a noun, as in *les amis* ('the friends'), or a pronoun and a verb, as in *Ils arrivent* ('They are coming'), form a phonological phrase. One can then argue that Liaison must apply within phonological phrases: [lezami] (*les amis*) and [izaʁiv] (*Ils arrivent*). But Liaison can be said to be blocked at the boundary between phonological phrases, as in the sentence *Les amis arrivent*, which can be said to consist of two phonological phrases: [*Les amis*] and [*arrivent*], pronounced [lezamiaʁiv], with no [z] at the end of the word *amis*. Phonologists who postulate units such as the phonological phrase often embrace the claim that syntactic structure does not directly trigger phonological processes; rather, certain syntactic configurations in specific languages are said to form phonological phrases, which then act as the **domain** for the application of certain phonological processes.

phonological word A **prosodic unit** postulated by some phonologists. It is claimed by some that this unit acts as the **domain** for the operation of certain phonological **processes**. It has been claimed that the phonological word in French consists of a **root** plus any suffixes which follow it, and that prefixes in French constitute separate phonological words. The process of **glide formation** in French is claimed to apply within phonological words, as in the adjective *colonial* ('colonial'), pronounced [kɔlɔnjal], derived from the noun *colonie* ('colony'), pronounced [kɔlɔni]. Here, the [i] at the end of *colonie* becomes the glide [j] when followed by a vowel-initial suffix, which forms a phonological word with the root. Glide formation fails to occur across the boundary between phonological words, as can be seen in the pronunciation of *Je vis à Paris* ('I live in Paris'), pronounced [ʒəviapaʁi]. Here, the [i] at the end of the phonological word *Je vie* does not undergo glide formation: the pronunciation is not [ʒəvjapaʁi].

phonologisation The term is used when 'low-level', universal phonetic tendencies attain the status of phonological generalisations in a specific language. Universally, vowels tend to be longer before **voiced** consonants. But this tendency can evolve into a **language-specific** vowel lengthening **process**, such as the **Scottish Vowel Length Rule,** in which specific vowels are considerably lengthened before specific voiced consonants.

The term is also used to describe the historical process by which a speech sound type changes its status from that of an **allophone** to that of the **realisation** of an independent **phoneme**. In present-day French, there is a /ʃ/ phoneme, as in words like /maʁʃe/ (*marcher*, 'to walk'). We can tell this because there are **minimal pairs** such as /maʁʃe/ vs /maʁke/ (*marquer*, 'to mark'). In **Old French**, there was no /ʃ/ phoneme; the [ʃ] sound was merely an allophone of the /k/ phoneme (*marcher* comes from the **Vulgar Latin** verb *marcare*, with a /k/), but it attained phonemic status during the evolution of the French phonemic system. This kind of phonologisation is also an example of a phonemic **split**.

phonology The study of the sound systems found in human languages. Some define phonology as the study of the functions of speech sounds. On that definition, phonology is functional **phonetics**. Others have a more **mentalistic** conception of what the discipline of phonology is; they see sound systems as being objects represented in the minds of human beings.

The term is used both for the discipline and for the object of inquiry; we talk of phonology as a field of study, parallel to politics, but as with the term 'politics', we also use the word 'phonology' to refer to the sound systems under investigation, as in the phrase 'Vowel harmony occurs in the phonology of Hungarian.'

The distinction and relation between phonology and phonetics is controversial. See **phoneme, Phonemic Principle** and **realisation**.

phonotactic constraints These are restrictions on the sequence of sounds that can occur in a given position in a **syllable**. They vary from one language to another. For instance, in most varieties of English, there are **constraints** on what kinds of consonant can occur in the first and second positions in a **branching onset**. If a **stop** consonant occupies the first slot in a branching onset, then only one of the following **approximants** can occur in the second position: /r, l, w, j/, as in *tray*, *play*, *twice* and *cure*. In contrast, French phonotactic constraints allow the consonants /n/ and /s/ in the second position in a branching onset, as in *pneu* ('tyre'), pronounced [pnø], and *psychiatre* ('psychia-trist'), pronounced [psikjatʁ]. Phonotactic constraints can refer to specific consonant types, as we have seen, but they can be very broad too. For instance, if a language allows only CV syllables, i.e. does not allow **coda** consonants, then that too would constitute a phonotactic constraint.

phrasal phonology see **Lexical Phonology**

phrasal stress Prominence of specific **syllables** in specific words in a phrase. In English, the phrasal stress rule is said to make the final element in the phrase the most prominent. In the noun phrase *tall boy*, the noun *boy* is most prominent. In the verb phrase *quickly departed*, the verb *departed* is most prominent. In the adjective phrase *very tall*, the adjective *tall* is most prominent. The application of the phrasal stress rule is said to trigger **Iambic Reversal**. In the word *thirteen*, *-teen* is normally more prominent than *thir-*. But when *thirteen* is inserted into a phrase such as *thirteen men*, the phrasal stress rule is said to create a stress clash between *men* and *-teen*, resulting in the reversal of the prominence patterns between *thir-* and *-teen*.

Piaget, Jean Twentieth-century Swiss psychologist who worked on child development. Unlike **Chomsky**, he argued that the child's linguistic development was integrated into the child's general **cognitive** development. Present-day Neo-Piagetians include Annette **Karmiloff-Smith**.

pidgin A pidgin language is a form of language which emerges when speakers of different languages seek to communicate. A pidgin language therefore acts as a

lingua franca. Some of the best-known examples are pidgin varieties of English, Dutch, French, Spanish and Portuguese which emerged during the slave trade. Pidgin languages are said to be syntactically, morphologically and phonologically simpler than the languages they are based on, which are the languages of the slave traders and the languages of the slaves. See **creole.**

Pierrehumbert, Janet An American phonologist known for her work on **intonation.** Pierrehumbert is a leading light in the **Laboratory Phonology** community, and is a proponent of **stochastic phonology.**

pitch The acoustic effect produced by different rates of vibration of the **vocal cords.** Generally speaking, the higher the rate of vibration, the higher the pitch. Pitch changes feature in **word stress, intonation and tone.**

pitch accent A form of **salience. Syllables** which have a **pitch** accent have pitch movement on that syllable, as in the Japanese word *toshokan* ('library') which has a sequence of three syllables, the first having a low pitch, the second a high pitch and the third a low pitch.

pitch accent language A language such as Japanese, in which each word has a single tonal pattern. In the Japanese word *toshokan* ('library'), the second syllable, with the high pitch, is the stressed syllable; the stress is conveyed by pitch alone, unlike in English. Pitch accent languages are said by many to be different from **tone languages** and **stress and intonation** languages.

place of articulation The point in the **oral cavity** at which a sound is articulated. For consonants, the main places of articulation are **labial, coronal** and **dorsal.**

plosive A synonym for a **stop**. See degree of **stricture**.

point vowels see **dispersion theory**

polysyllabic Containing more than two **syllables**. The English words *elephant*, *elaborate* and *gentlemanliness* are all polysyllabic.

polysystemic Polysystemic approaches to the nature of phonological contrasts differ from the classical **phonemic** approach. Under the latter, one considers the entire set of **environments**, and establishes **allophones** on the basis of **complementary distribution**. On this view, there is a single set of phonemic **oppositions**, with the allophones of those phonemes being distributed across a range of environments. On the polysystemic approach, one postulates several sets of phonemic systems for *each* environment, such as **onset** position and **coda** position. On this view, a given language has, for example, a system of onset consonants and a distinct system of coda consonants. Associated with the work of British linguist J. R. **Firth**.

postalveolar Sounds which are postalveolar are produced with a stricture involving the **blade** of the tongue and the area just behind the **alveolar ridge**. Examples are the English **fricatives** in words such as *ship* [ʃɪp] and *measure* [mɛʒə]. Many phonologists and phoneticians still use the term **palato-alveolar** for such sounds, though this does not feature in the most recent revision of the **IPA**.

postvocalic Occurring after a **vowel**. The /d/ in the word *bad* is postvocalic.

Poverty of the Stimulus (POS) argument see **stimulus**

Prague School A group of linguists and philosophers, based in Prague from the mid-1920s into the 1930s, who developed several concepts in linguistic analysis, including **markedness** and the idea of different types of phonological **opposition**. Perhaps the best-known phonologist working in the Prague School was a Russian prince called Nikolaj **Trubetzkoy**. The phonologist Roman **Jakobson** also worked closely with members of the Prague School.

pre-aspirated stops Stops which are pre-aspirated have a period of **aspiration** preceding the stop closure, as in the case of the [ht] stop found in Icelandic. These are distinct from post-aspirated stops such as the [pʰ], [tʰ] and [kʰ] in English, which are normally referred to simply as aspirated stops. Icelandic has both pre-aspirated and post-aspirated stops. In some languages, such as the Applecross dialect of Scots Gaelic, pre-aspirated stops have been analysed as single **contour segments**. In other languages, such as Icelandic, they are analysed as sequences of two **segments**.

prenasalised stops Stops which are treated as single **segments**, but which contain a **nasal** articulation prior to the **oral stop** articulation, as in the Terena word [mbiho] ('I went'). Prenasalised stops, like **affricates**, are often described as **contour segments**, or complex segments, since, in each case, there are two distinct, sequential subparts within a single segment.

pre-pausal Occurring before a pause. The [t] at the end of the utterance 'He got hit' is in pre-pausal position if the speaker pauses at the end of that utterance.

prevocalic Occurring before a **vowel**. The [ɹ] in the sentence *I'm ready* is in prevocalic position.

primary articulation The main articulation produced in sounds which also have a **secondary articulation**. The primary articulation in English 'dark l' is **alveolar**, but this sound also has a secondary articulation, a **velarisation** in which the **back of the tongue** articulates with the **velum**.

primary stress Some languages have more than one degree of **word stress**. Many varieties of English are said to have both *primary stress* and *secondary stress*, as in the word *preconception*, which contains both a secondary stress and a primary stress: [ˌpreconˈception], where the **diacritic** [ˌ] marks secondary stress, and the diacritic [ˈ] marks primary stress. The idea is that the **syllables** between the stressed syllables are unstressed, and thus less prominent than the stressed syllables, but that the syllable with primary stress is more prominent than the syllable with secondary stress.

Prince, Alan An American phonologist who works within the **generative phonology** tradition. He is known for his work in **Metrical Phonology**. He is considered the co-founder, with Paul **Smolensky**, of **Optimality Theory**. He has also worked with John **McCarthy** on Optimality Theory.

principles Many linguists believe that there are basic principles which govern the structure of human languages. In the field of phonology, **avoidance of homophony** is considered to be a functioning general principle, which is said to come into conflict with the tendency towards **ease of articulation**.

A more formal sense of 'principle' is used in branches of **generative linguistics** which postulate formal principles and **parameters**, given by **Universal Grammar**.

principles and parameters approach Any approach to the theory of linguistic structure which postulates linguistic **principles** and **parameters** that are said to be given by **Universal Grammar**. Mostly associated with syntactic analyses adopted within present-day **generative linguistics**, but the notion has been adopted by generative phonologists.

privative feature A **feature** which is said to be either present or absent, as in the case of the feature [labial], present in segments such as /u/, /o/, /p/, /b/ and /m/, but absent in segments such as /i/, /e/, /t/, /d/ and /n/. See also **opposition**.

privative opposition see **opposition**

process One way of talking about the relationship between related phonetic and phonological forms is to appeal to the idea of phonetic or phonological processes. In Korean, there are related forms, such as [pap] ('cooked rice') and [pabi] (the 'subjective' form of the 'cooked rice' morpheme). Phonologists have analysed such pairs by postulating an **underlying representation** of the form /pap/, with an underlyingly **voiceless unaspirated stop**. Forms such as [pabi] are then said to result from the operation of a process of **intervocalic voicing**. The process idea tends to be associated with the notion of phonological *rule*.

proclitic see **clitic**

productivity The extent to which a given phonological, morphological or syntactic pattern can apply to create new forms. The suffix -*ee* in contemporary English is currently exhibiting a certain degree of productivity;

speakers are uttering new forms such as *kissee* and *teachee*, in which the new forms denote the person undergoing the experience. It is claimed, particularly in **usage-based phonology**, that the productivity of a given pattern is largely determined by the **type frequency** of the pattern.

progressive (preservative) assimilation see **assimilation**

prominence A synonym of **salience**.

proparoxytone A word which has **primary stress** on the **antepenultimate** syllable, as in the English word *America*.

prosodic Relating to **prosody**.

prosodic domains see **prosodic hierarchy**

prosodic hierarchy It is often claimed that phonological units larger than the **segment** form a hierarchy of ever-larger units, known as the prosodic hierarchy. An example of such a proposed hierarchy would contain the units known as the **syllable**, the **foot**, the **phonological word**, the **phonological phrase**, the **intonational phrase** and the **utterance**. As one moves from the syllable at the bottom of the hierarchy to the utterance at the top, the units are said to get larger, so that feet contain syllables, phonological words contain feet, and so on. It is a moot point whether all languages have all of these units. It is also debatable whether utterances can be strictly subdivided into neat packages containing such units.

Prosodic Morphology An approach to **morphology**, associated primarily with the work of John **McCarthy** and

Alan **Prince**, in which morphological **templates** are said to be definable in terms of **prosodic constituents** such as the **syllable** and the metrical **foot**.

prosody The study of prosody is the study of **suprasegmental features** of speech, such as **word stress, rhythm** and **intonation**. Some phonologists treat other phenomena, such as **nasality**, as a potentially prosodic property. The term is used in **Firthian Phonology** to denote phonological elements which correspond to what were later called autosegments. See **Autosegmental Phonology**.

proto-language A reconstructed earlier stage in the history of a **language family**. Examples are Proto-Indo-European, the reconstructed precursor of the **Indo-European** language family and Proto-Dravidian, the reconstructed precursor of the present-day **Dravidian** languages, such as Malayalam, Tamil and Telugu.

The term 'proto-language' is also used by the linguist Derek Bickerton to refer to a postulated more 'primitive' form of human language which he claims was an evolutionary precursor to fully-fledged human language.

prototypes In the work of Eleanor Rosch, it is argued that human perception relies heavily on prototypes, which are central exemplars of a given category. In the field of colour perception, it is said that we have a clear sense of a prototypical example of, say, 'green', and a prototypical example of, say, 'blue'. But we are poor at categorising tokens which lie on the fuzzy boundaries of blueness and greenness, and will often disagree as to whether a given object is green or blue, if the colour is not prototypical. It is argued that vowel perception works in the same way. Native speakers are good at recognising a prototypical example of, say, /ɪ/ in English, as in the word *pit*; they are also good at recognising prototypical examples of /ɛ/, as in the word *pet*. But if we hear non-prototypical exemplars of these **phonemes**, articulated halfway between /ɪ/ and /ɛ/, we are less good at identifying the vowel sound (though context of utterance will help immensely in guessing what word is intended).

Prototypes are said by some to be central to speech perception and to our conceptual categories, so that concepts such as 'dog' are said to have more and less central exemplars. Prototype theory is similar to **exemplar theory**.

psychological reality The idea that the phonological representations and generalisations postulated by linguists correspond in some way to mental entities and/or processes in the minds of speaker/hearers. See **realism**.

pull chain A synonym for a **drag chain**. See **vowel shift**.

Pullum, Geoffrey A British linguist who spent a great deal of his career in the USA before returning to Britain in 2007 to become Professor of Linguistics at Edinburgh University in Scotland. Pullum's early work was on **SPE phonology**, but he has worked on a remarkably wide range of areas in linguistics, including syntactic theory (he was one of the co-founders of a framework known as Generalised Phrase Structure Grammar) and the syntax-phonology interface. He is co-author of a phonetic symbol guide and lately known for his work with the philosopher Barbara Scholz criticising the **Poverty of the Stimulus argument** and, more generally, Chomsky's **Rationalism**.

pulmonic egressive see **airstream mechanisms**

pulmonic ingressive see **airstream mechanisms**

push chain see **vowel shift**

Q

quantity A property often attributed to **syllables**, normally the **rhyme** of the syllable. Syllables are often said to be **heavy** if the rhyme contains a certain amount of phonological material. Syllable rhymes in Latin are said to have been **light** if they contained only a **short** vowel, and heavy if they contained a **long** vowel, a **diphthong**, or a vowel followed by a **coda** consonant. The heavy syllables are said to have greater quantity than the light syllables. In the Latin word *l[a]udati* ('praised'), pronounced [lauda:ti], the final syllable is light and the other two syllables are heavy. Many **word** stress systems are said to be governed by syllable quantity. In Latin, words which are **trisyllabic** or longer are said to have been stressed on the **penultimate** syllable if it was heavy, or otherwise on the **antepenultimate** syllable. Some phonologists distinguish quantity as a phonological property from **length** as a purely phonetic property of **segments**.

quantity sensitivity A term for **word stress** assignment systems in which **syllable weight** (otherwise known as syllable **quantity**) plays a role.

R

'r' sounds Otherwise known as **rhotics**. It is common for phonologists to postulate different 'r' sounds in a language, and the range of sounds considered to be 'r' sounds is remarkably broad, subsuming **taps**, **trills**, **fricatives** and **approximants**. It is a moot point whether there is a **natural class** of 'r' sounds. It is worth noting that, although the class of sounds considered to be rhotics is large, it is none the less constrained; no **nasal stops** ever count as rhotics, for example, and nor do **voiceless stops**.

radical consonants Sequences of three **consonants** in Arabic which constitute morphological **roots**. **Vowels** can then be interspersed among these consonants, and various **affixes** can be added to them. The sequence /drs/ is an example. With the addition of various vowels and affixes, the following forms, among others, can be created: [darasa] ('he studied', [darsun] ('a lesson'), [madrasah] ('Koranic school'). In the analysis of such forms, phonologists often appeal to the idea of **templates** such as CVCVC, found in the first example.

Radoppiamento Sintattico (RS) Literally, 'syntactic doubling'. An **external sandhi** phenomenon found in Italian, in which a **word-initial** consonant undergoes **gemination** (doubling) next to a word boundary, as in *Era venuto con tré piccoli cani* ('He came with three little dogs'), in which the underlyingly **short** [p] in *piccoli* (the plural form of the adjective meaning 'little') is geminated to [pp]. The **process** applies if the **segment** following the target consonant is a **vowel**, a **liquid** or a **glide**, and if the **syllable** preceding the target consonant is stressed. There has been much discussion of the conditions for RS. Like Liaison in French, it does not happen across all sequences of two words, and this has led to discussion as to whether syntactic structure plays a direct role in the triggering of the process, or whether there is an indirect link between syntactic structure and phonological processes, mediated by postulated units such as the **phonological phrase**.

raised A vowel is said to be raised if its articulation has moved upwards in the **vowel space**. In the **Northern Cities Vowel Shift**, many of the articulations of the /æ/ **phoneme** are raised towards the **low mid** vowel [ɛ], or even higher than that.

raising Any phonological **process** in which vowels are raised in the **vowel space**. An example is **DRESS Raising** in New Zealand English, in which vowels of the **lexical set** DRESS are raised from the **low mid** [ɛ] position and pronounced as [ɪ], as in the pronunciation of the word *desk* as [dɪsk]. Raising in phonology is not to be confused with the use of the same term in the history of generative syntax.

Rationalism A tradition in the history of philosophy which rests on the idea that certain kinds of **cognitive** content are native to, or innate in, the human mind and not acquired via interaction with the environment. It is important not to confuse this meaning with the everyday use of the term, which means 'relying on rationality'. Rationalism is associated with the work of the French philosopher Descartes, who argued that the human mind is possessed, at birth, with certain 'innate ideas'. The notion of innate cognitive content was pursued in the twentieth century by **Chomsky**, who claims that humans are born with innate linguistic knowledge, including phonological knowledge. Rationalism is often referred to as **Nativism**. The idea that humans are born with innate linguistic knowledge is opposed by those who support **Empiricism**.

Innate phonological knowledge is said to include general principles governing the shape of the phonological systems of human languages.

Rationalist Relating to **Rationalism**.

realisation A term often used by scholars who postulate a distinction between phonological and phonetic representations, and who see the relation between the two to be one of the phonological representation being realised in phonetic substance. The term is somewhat unfortunate for proponents of **realism,** since it suggests that the phonological representation is somehow less real than the phonetic representation, but this is usually not intended by authors who use the term. Other terms used to designate the relation between **phonology** and **phonetics** are manifestation, phonetic **implementation**, phonetic **interpretation** and phonetic **exponence.** Others use the term **transduction** to describe the relationship between phonology and phonetics phonological objects, taken to be **mental** in nature, are said to be transduced into phonetic substance. It is, at times, unclear exactly what terms such as these are supposed to mean. There is no consensus on whether a clear distinction can be drawn between phonology and phonetics, and even those who believe that such a distinction can be drawn do not agree on how it should be drawn, or on what the relation between the two is.

realisational difference A difference between two varieties of a language is said to be realisational if there is a difference in the way the **phonemes** of those varieties are realised. In **Received Pronunciation** (RP), the /l/ phoneme is realised as a 'dark l' in the **rhyme** of a syllable, as in the word *dull*: [dʌɫ], where the /l/ is in the **coda** position of the rhyme. In the word *lip*, the /l/ is in the **onset**, and is therefore not realised as a dark l in RP. The word *lull* in RP has an /l/ in onset position and an /l/ in the rhyme, and is therefore pronounced [lʌɫ], with two different l sounds. In **Standard Scottish English**, the /l/ phoneme is realised as a dark l in all syllabic positions, so that *lull* is pronounced [ɫʌɫ]. This kind of difference is realisational, not systemic; the difference does not lie in the set of phonemic **oppositions** found in the two varieties, but in the way a specific phoneme is realised. See **systemic differences**.

realism A way of interpreting scientific theories, according to which the theoretical constructs postulated by the scientist are assumed to correspond to real entities and events. A realist interpretation of atomic theory assumes that atoms are real. Adopting a realist interpretation of phonological constructs such as **phoneme**, **syllable** and **foot** means assuming that such things are real entities in some sense. The alternative to this assumption is to adopt an **instrumentalist** interpretation of theoretical constructs, according to which we are not justified in assuming that phonemes, feet, syllables and other postulated objects actually exist outside of our theories.

Received Pronunciation (RP) An **accent** of English which has often been associated with speakers who attended the English fee-paying schools. It is widely taught to foreign learners of English around the world. Some phonologists prefer to speak of the present-day RP-type accents as Standard Southern British English. RP is also referred to as **BBC English**, although BBC presenters nowadays speak with a wide variety of accents.

reciprocal assimilation see **assimilation**

recursion In syntax, a syntactic category is said to be recursive if one can identify an instance of that category occurring within a category of the same type. For instance, the noun phrase, *The old man in the park*, contains another noun phrase (*the park*). Since noun phrases can occur within noun phrases in English, we say that noun phrase is a **recursive** category in English. It has often been claimed that recursion is a universal property of human language, present in all human languages. This claim has recently been disputed by the linguist Dan **Everett**. Recursive categories have been postulated in phonology, but their status is much more questionable than the status of recursive categories in syntax. Examples of postulated recursive categories in phonology are the **phonological word** and the **intonational phrase**.

recursive see **recursion**

reduced vowel see **reduction**

reduction With respect to **consonants**, this is a **process** in which a sound with **oral cavity** articulation comes to be replaced by another sound without oral cavity articulation. **Voiceless fricatives** are often historically reduced to **glottal** fricatives, with loss of **stricture** in the oral cavity. Spanish *hijo* ('son') used to be pronounced with an [h] at an earlier stage in the history of the language. This [h] was a reduced form of Latin [f] in *filium*. Voiceless **oral stops** are often reduced to **glottal stops**, again with loss of stricture in the oral cavity, as in the pronunciation [bʌʔə] (*butter*). This process is often called **glottalling**. With respect to **vowels**, in many languages, unstressed vowels are often reduced to **schwa,** which involves no deviation from the **neutral position of the tongue.** A word such as *personal* has **reduced vowels** in its unstressed syllables, both of them schwas: ['pʰɜːsənəl], but in the word *personality*, the syllable with **primary stress** has a non-reduced vowel: [ˌpʰɜːsə'nælɪti]. Some languages have a more restricted range of vowel phonemes in unstressed syllables than is found in stressed syllables, but none the less do not reduce the unstressed vowels to schwa. In Catalan, the seven vowels /i, e, ɛ, a, ɔ, o, u/ can occur in stressed syllables, but in unstressed syllables only /i, a, u/ can occur. This kind of phenomenon is analysed as a kind of vowel reduction by some.

redundancy see **redundant**

redundant A phonetic feature is said to be redundant if its occurrence is predictable from context. The notion is central to the **Phonemic Principle: allophonic** properties of speech sounds are predictable from context, as in the case of the **intervocalic voicing** of **unaspirated voiceless stops** in Korean, where **morphemes** such as /pap/ ('cooked rice') have a [b] realisation of the morpheme-final /p/ in forms such as [pabi]. In **SPE phonology, underlying representations** were stripped of all such redundant features, so that the underlying representation for 'cooked rice' in Korean would be /pap/.

In **exemplar theory,** it is argued that mental representations of words are not stripped of redundant phonetic material but are stored in the form they are heard, with all the phonetic detail which was perceived when a word was uttered on a specific occasion.

reduplication A **morphological process** in which segmental material from a **base** is copied. In Maori, /mate/

means 'sick' and the reduplicated form /matemate/ means 'sickly'. Reduplication is relevant for phonology because any account of reduplication phenomena requires a statement of exactly which phonological material is to be reduplicated. There are clear cases, such as our Maori example, in which a **constituent** such as a syllable or a word is reduplicated. But other reduplication phenomena are less straightforward, leading phonologists to appeal to notions such as **templates** and **underspecification**. In Ilokano, a Philippine language, the progressive form of the base [basa] ('read') is [ag+bas+basa], with [bas] copied from the base. Here, what is copied is neither a syllable nor a base. The same is true for the base [trabaho] ('work'), whose reduplicated form is [ag+trab+trabaho]. An analysis making appeal to the idea of a template would postulate a prefix consisting of a CCVC template which is underspecified for phonological content. Segmental content from the base is then copied on to the template. Other phonologists have argued that there are **prosodic** constraints on reduplication, so that the reduplicated material is a prosodic constituent such as the **mora,** the **syllable** and the **foot**. In the case of Ilokano reduplication, the suggestion is that the sequence CCVC is not arbitrary, but corresponds to the language's maximal syllable.

regressive (anticipatory) assimilation see **assimilation**

Rendaku A well-known **voicing process** in Japanese, in which an initial **voiceless** consonant in a compound becomes **voiced** when inserted into the compound. The standard example is the combination or *ori* ('fold') plus *kami* ('paper'), which together form the compound [origami] ('paper folding'). See **Lyman's Law**.

repair strategies An idea associated with the work of Canadian phonologist Carole **Paradis**. In her theory of **constraints** and repair strategies, both universal and **language-specific** constraints are postulated. When these are violated, repair strategies may be triggered. For instance, if a given language has a language-specific constraint prohibiting adjacent consonants, then any such sequence could be repaired by the insertion of an **epenthetic** vowel between the two consonants.

representation A notion that has been widely appealed to in phonology in a variety of different ways. In **SPE phonology**, a distinction was made between two significant levels of phonological representation, both attributed with **psychological reality**. The first was the level of **systematic phonemic/phonological representation**, otherwise known as **underlying representation**. This was a level at which all **redundant** (predictable) phonetic features were stripped away. Those features were then supplied by phonological **rules**, which yielded a **derived** level of representation known as the **systematic phonetic level of representation**.

resonance chamber Any of the three chambers in the **vocal tract** in which resonance may take place: the **oral cavity**, the **nasal cavity** and the **pharynx**.

resyllabification see **syllable**

retracted see **vowel retraction**

Retracted Tongue Root (RTR) A property often associated with **vowels**, in which the **root** of the tongue is retracted, resulting in various effects on the **body of the**

tongue. Typical RTR and non-RTR vowel pairs are [i]/[ɪ], [u]/[ʊ], [e]/[ɛ], [o]/[ɔ], in which the latter member is RTR. Such pairs often figure in **vowel harmony** systems. There is often debate as to whether a given system is **ATR**-based or RTR-based. It appears that ATR-based systems may change into RTR systems over time. Some believe that there are languages with both ATR and RTR vowel harmony.

retraction see **vowel retraction** and **stress retraction**

retroflex A speech sound is said to be retroflex when the **tip/blade** of the tongue is curled back and the underside of the tip/blade forms a constriction with the **passive articulator**, usually the **alveolar ridge**. Retroflex consonants are common in both the **Dravidian** and the **Indo-European** languages of India, such as Tamil. They include retroflex **stops**, such as the **voiceless** retroflex stop [ʈ] in the Tamil word [ʈaβam] ('penance'), and the **voiced** retroflex stop [ɖ] in the Tamil word [puːɳɖʊ] ('garlic'). The latter word also contains the retroflex **nasal stop** [ɳ]. The Tamil word [kuʈʊ] ('give') contains the retroflex **tap/flap** [ɽ], and the Tamil word [paʐɯ] ('waste') contains the voiced retroflex **fricative** [ʐ].

reversal see **Iambic Reversal**

rhotic A language, or variety of a language, is said to be rhotic if its '**r**' **sounds** may appear in both **onsets** and **codas**. In **Standard Scottish English** and in many varieties of American English, an 'r' is pronounced in *farm* and *far left*. See **non-rhotic**.

rhotics see '**r**' **sounds**

rhyme There are two different senses of this word.

There is a phenomenon known as rhyme which is found in poetry and song. In English, the unit for rhyming is the **metrical foot**, with any **onset** consonants ignored, so that *city* rhymes with *witty*. Each word constitutes a **trochaic** metrical foot, and when one ignores the onset consonants, both have the foot [ɪti]. Because metrical feet can cut across word boundaries, it is possible to form rhymes such as the following: *pneumonia* and *stone ya* (informal spelling of *stone you*, as in the sentence *They'll stone ya.*) The word *pneumonia* has an initial unstressed syllable, followed by the metrical foot [məʊnjə]. The phrase *stone ya* consists of the metrical foot [stəʊnjə]. Ignoring the onset consonants, both expressions contain the metrical foot [əʊnjə], and thus they rhyme. Popular music abounds with examples like this.

The term is also used to refer to a **constituent** within a **syllable** which consists of the **nucleus** and any **coda** consonants. It is worth noting that, despite its name, the rhyme of a syllable is not the basis for rhyming in English. See **syllable**.

rhythm The regular placement of beats in speech. While all human speech is rhythmic, different human languages exhibit different rhythmic patterns. One pattern contains a perceptually salient syllable followed by a less salient syllable, as in the English word *father*. Such a structure is known as a **trochee**, and is referred to as a **trochaic** structure. Another pattern contains a less salient syllable followed by a more salient one, as in the word [ŋin'tip] ('bee') in the language Weri. This is known as an **iamb**, and is referred to as an **iambic** structure. The structures in question are often referred to as **metrical feet**. It is said that

English *father* constitutes a trochaic foot, while Weri *ŋintip* constitues an iambic foot. The most prominent syllable in a foot may have only **secondary stress**, as in the English word *preconception*, which contains two trochaic feet: [ˌprecon] [ˈception].

rhythm rule see **Iambic Reversal**

right-headed Used to refer to phonological **constituents** in which the **head** is located at the right edge of the constituent, as in the case of **iambic feet**. These can be found in, for example, the South American language Weri. An example from this language is the word [ŋinˈtip] ('bee'), in which the final stressed syllable forms an iambic foot with the preceding unstressed syllable. See **left-headed** and **rhythm**.

rising diphthong A **diphthong** in which the most prominent element is the second, as French [wa] ('goose'), where the [a] is more prominent than the **on-glide** [w]. The most prominent element in a diphthong is often referred to as the **head** of the diphthong.

Romance languages A subgrouping within the **Indo-European language family** which includes present-day languages such as Catalan, French, Italian, Occitan, Portuguese and Spanish. The Romance languages are historically derived from **Vulgar Latin**.

root A term from the field of **morphology**, designating the part of a word which remains once all **affixes** have been removed. For instance, in the English word *unfriendliness*, once one removes the prefix *un-* and the suffixes *-ly* and *-ness*, one arrives at the root *friend*. The term is also used in **phonetics** to refer to the **tongue root**.

rounded Having lip-rounding. **Back** vowels are typically rounded, as in the case of [u] and [o], but there are **front** rounded vowels too, as in the case of the French vowels [y], [ø] and [œ] found in the words *lune* ('moon'), *peu* ('little') and *sœur* ('sister'). Consonants can also have lip-rounding, as in the case of the English **palato-alveolar** sound [ʃ], found in words such as *share* and *ash*.

roundedness The property of being **rounded**. For some phonologists working with **private features**, roundedness is subsumed under **labiality**

RP see **Received Pronunciation**

RTR see **Retracted Tongue Root**

rule A way of stating a generalisation. When we say that there is a rule of **voicing assimilation** in Polish, this is a way of saying that there is a generalisation to be made about the assimilation that occurs between adjacent **obstruents** in Polish. An alternative way of stating the generalisation would be in the form of a **constraint**.

rule-governed A given phonological pattern is said to be **rule**-governed if it exhibits a clearly stateable regularity. The occurrence of the **allophones** of a **phoneme** are said to be rule-governed if we can state exactly which **environments** they occur in. The **word stress** patterns of a language are said to be rule-governed if we can state an explicit **algorithm** for word stress assignment in that language.

Rutgers Optimality Archive (ROA) An on-line archive of papers on **Optimality Theory**, based at Rutgers University in the USA.

S

salience A perceptual notion. In all languages, some phonological units will be more salient (prominent) to its speakers than others. Stressed **syllables** are more salient than unstressed syllables, as in the word *happen*, where the **penultimate** syllable is more salient than the final syllable. Among the stressed syllables, syllables bearing the **tonic** are more salient than syllables which do not carry the tonic, as in *Mary bought a dress*, in which the tonic syllable *dress* is more salient than the other stressed syllables *Mary* and *bought*.

Sampson, Geoffrey A British linguist who has consistently opposed the **Rationalist** belief that humans are born with linguistic knowledge. In opposition to this, Sampson claims that we learn the language(s) we speak, using general learning mechanisms. Sampson supports **Empiricism**; he denies the existence of **Universal Grammar**. While he has not worked on phonology, his views are relevant for the study of phonology. According to his view, human children learn the phonology of their language from scratch; there is no innate phonological knowledge (though this is not to deny that humans possess certain innate perceptual and articulatory capacities).

sandhi A term taken from **Sanskrit**, meaning 'putting together', from *sam* ('together') and *dhi*, ('put'). The term was first used by the ancient Indian grammarians. Sandhi **processes** are processes which operate across morphological and syntactic boundaries. **External sandhi** processes operate across word boundaries. The phenomenon of **Linking 'r'** in **non-rhotic** varieties of English, as in [fɑːɹəweɪ], *far away*, is an example of this, since the presence of the 'r' is triggered by the presence of a vowel-initial word following the word *far*. **Internal sandhi** processes operate within word boundaries often across **morpheme boundaries**, as in the case of Lumasaaba morphemes such as /li/ ('a root'), realised as [di] when a **nasal stop** precedes it, as in the form [zindi] ('roots'). Some processes operate both internally and externally, sometimes beginning as internal sandhi, and then being extended such that they also operate externally.

Sanskrit An **Indo-European** language which was spoken on the Indian subcontinent. The present-day Indo-European languages of India, such as Bengali and Hindi, are said to be descendants of Sanskrit. It was the discovery of systematic phonological and morphological relationships between Sanskrit, Latin and Ancient Greek that led to the postulating of the Indo-European **language family**.

Sapir, Edward (1884–1939) An American linguist who did a great deal of work on native American Indian languages in the first half of the twentieth century. He studied with **Boas**, and is known for his combination of anthropological linguistics and **mentalism**. Sapir stressed the cultural, as opposed to biological, nature of linguistic practices. Unlike some of his American successors in the mid-twentieth century, he was committed to the **psychological reality** of phonological representations. His name is also associated with the 'Sapir-Whorf Hypothesis' because of his association with Benjamin Lee Whorf and the idea that the language one has learned shapes the kinds of thought process in which we regularly engage.

Saussure, Ferdinand de (1857–1913) A Swiss linguist often described as 'the father of modern linguistics', and frequently associated with various versions of **Structuralism**. He was concerned to identify what the object of linguistic inquiry was, and argued that it was **langue**, a system of linguistic **signs**, as opposed to **parole**, often referred to as the physical realisation of the underlying system. The distinction between langue and parole bears some similarity to **Chomsky**'s distinction between **competence** and **performance**, but, for Saussure, langue is said to be a social fact, whereas Chomsky takes competence to reside in individuals, not in a social collectivity. The linguistic sign, for Saussure, was an arbitrary connection between a phonological representation (for Saussure, this was said to be an acoustic image) and a concept. But if acoustic images and concepts exist in individual minds, rather than in a social collectivity, it is hard to see how the social concept of langue can be sustained. Linguistic signs were said by Saussure to stand in **opposition** to each other. Saussure also distinguished between the **synchronic** and the **diachronic** study of language. His emphasis on the importance of synchronic linguistics influenced the way linguistics was practised in the twentieth century. He is best known for the *Course in General Linguistics*, published in French in 1916. Unfortunately, the book was not actually written by Saussure; it is a reconstruction of lecture notes taken by two of his students. There is a large literature on how to interpret Saussure's ideas, and on decisions taken by different translators as to how best to translate key terms from the *Course in General Linguistics* into English.

Schane, Sanford An American phonologist who was the first to investigate the phonology of French within the

SPE phonology framework. He later developed an approach to phonological segments, known as Particle Phonology, based on the notion of **elements**.

schwa The name for a **vowel quality** which is produced without lip rounding and with the **body of the tongue** in the **neutral position**. Transcribed as [ə], it occurs widely in unstressed syllables in many varieties of English, as in the word *character*: [ˈkʰæɹəktə]. This vowel **alternates** with a wide variety of other vowels in many languages. It also alternates with **zero** in many languages, such as French.

Scots A language spoken in Scotland, Canada and Northern Ireland which is derived historically from the Northumbrian dialect of **Old English**. Scots is not to be confused with Scots Gaelic, which is a Celtic language spoken in Scotland and Canada. Nor is it to be confused with **Standard Scottish English**, the **accent** of English spoken predominantly by the educated middle classes in Scotland. Whether Scots is to be viewed as a **dialect** of English or as a separate language, as suggested here, is a sociopolitical issue. A few examples of Scots words are *bairn* ('child'), *lum* ('chimney') and the verb *fash* ('get annoyed'), as in the expression 'Dinnae fash yersel' ('Don't get irritated or upset').

Scottish Standard English see **Standard Scottish English**

Scottish Vowel Length Rule (SVLR) A **vowel lengthening process** in **Scots** and Scottish English whereby the vowels /i/, /u/ and /ʌi/ are lengthened before **voiced fricatives**, /r/ or a **morpheme boundary**, as in the words [biːz] (*bees*), [biːɹ] (*beer*) and [əgɹiːd] (*agreed*). Also known as **Aitken's Law**, after the linguist Jack Aitken.

secondary articulation see **primary articulation**

secondary stress see **primary stress**

segmental Relating to **segments**. Segmental phonology is the study of segmental phenomena such as vowel and consonant **allophones**.

segments Many phonologists argue that the continuous stream of speech is analysed by speakers into segments, which may group together to form **syllables,** so that the **monosyllabic** English word *bit* can be analysed as the sequence of segments [b]-[ɹ]-[t]. Some argue that segments are an artefact stemming from our knowledge of alphabetic writing systems. Others argue that the idea of segments is not a mere artefact, but that segments are **psychologically real** objects which enter into the speech planning process, and are reflected in **slip of the tongue** phenomena.

semiconsonant There is a class of **segments** which, like **vowels,** are **voiced** and have a stricture of **open approximation,** but which, unlike vowels, do not occupy the **head** position in the **nucleus** of a **syllable.** Examples are the [w] in *wet* and the [j] in *yet.* Also known as **semivowel.** See **glides** and **yod.**

Semitic A **language family** which includes Hebrew and the various dialects of Arabic.

semivowel Synonym for **semiconsonant.**

sentence The term is often used in its ordinary, everyday sense to denote a syntactic unit consisting of a subject and a predicate, as in the unit *John went to* *the pub*, where *John* is the subject and *went to the pub* is the predicate. It has been used more technically in the literature on **generative linguistics**, where a distinction has sometimes been drawn between the sentence as a unit of **competence** and the **utterance** as a unit of **performance**. The notion 'sentence' is sometimes used in phonology when discussing **sentence stress**.

sentence stress A term sometimes used to refer to the placement of the **tonic** in a sentence.

shibboleth Any feature of language use which betrays one's social or ethnic origins. Pronounced ['ʃɪbələθ], it derives from a Hebrew word which features in a biblical tale in which the members of an ethnic group are identified by their pronunciation of the word, and then slaughtered. Shibboleths can be syntactic, morphological or phonological. An example of a present-day phonological shibboleth in England is the pronunciation, by speakers with a North of England origin, of words of the sort *bath* and *class* with the **short** /æ/ **phoneme**, instead of the **long** /ɑː/ phoneme found in **Received Pronunciation (RP)** and similar accents. Since speakers from the North of England are sometimes associated with working-class lifestyles, uttering shibboleths of this sort can lead to such speakers being judged socially inferior.

short see **length**

shortening Any **process** in which a **segment** is shortened. An example is trisyllabic shortening.

sibilant harmony see **consonant harmony**

sign A term used by **Saussure** to denote the arbitrary coupling, in a given language, of an acoustic image and a concept, so that the English acoustic image represented by /dɒg/ is arbitrarily coupled, in English, with the concept 'dog'. Saussure described the acoustic image as a **signifier**, and described the concept as the **signified**. Unfortunately, many writers use the term 'sign' to denote actual sequences of speech sounds, such as the **utterance** [dɒg]. And many people use the term 'signified' to denote, for instance, the set of all dogs, rather than the concept 'dog'. This is arguably not what Saussure intended.

signified see **sign**

signifier see **sign**

slack vocal folds A **laryngeal** feature said to be present during the production of **voiced** sounds.

slanted brackets The brackets used to represent **phonemes**. See **square brackets** and **phonemic transcription**.

slip of the tongue A speech error, such as a **Spoonerism**. Slips of the tongue give us insights into articulatory planning and production. 'It's roaring with pain', instead of 'It's pouring with rain', is an example.

Smolensky, Paul An American scholar who works on **formalist** approaches to the study of human **cognition**. Smolensky has worked extensively on **neural nets** and is also known as the co-founder, with Alan **Prince**, of **Optimality Theory**.

smoothing An informal term for **monophthongisation**.

sociolinguistics The study of the relationship between language use and social context. Important for phonology, since the way people speak is intimately tied into their social background. Examples of sociolinguistic variables which affect the different ways in which people speak are age, social class, ethnicity and gender.

sociophonetic variation Variation in people's speech which is governed by sociolinguistic factors such as age, gender, ethnicity and social class. An example of this is the occurrence of a **pre-aspirated** pronunciation of [t] in **pre-pausal** position in **Tyneside English**; this pronunciation is correlated with age, social class and gender, since it is found predominantly among young working-class women.

soft palate see **velum**

sonorants A subset of the set of **consonants**. Consonants are often subdivided into **obstruents** and sonorants. The term subsumes **nasal stops**, such as [m] and [n], and **liquids**, such as [l] and [ɹ].

sonority hierarchy A hierarchy of classes of speech sound types, organised according to their degree of sonority. Two main factors determine how sonorous a sound is: the degree of obstruction of the **vocal tract** during the production of the sound, and whether the sound is **voiced** or not. **Oral stops** have a high degree of obstruction, the stricture of **complete closure**, and are thus less sonorant than **fricatives**. All voiced sounds are more sonorous than their **voiceless** counterparts, so that, within the class of **obstruents**, the hierarchy reads as follows: voiced fricatives>-

voiceless fricatives>voiced **stops**>voiceless stops, where '>' means 'more sonorant than'. The class of sonorant consonants (**sonorants**) are all considered more sonorant than the class of obstruents. Among the class of sonorants, there is disagreement as to which are more sonorous than others, but it is common to take **glides** to be more sonorant than **liquids**, which in turn are more sonorant than the **nasal stops** (nasals). The most sonorant of all classes are vowels, which have a structure of **open approximation** and are typically voiced. Among the vowels, the more open a vowel, the more sonorant it is, since openness equates with less obstruction in the vocal tract. A general depiction of the sonority hierarchy would be: vowels>glides>liquids>nasals>obstruents. The sonority hierarchy is said to figure in **processes** of **lenition**, with speech sounds becoming more sonorous as they are lenited. In processes of **fortition**, sounds are said to move up the sonority hierarchy, becoming less sonorous. The sonority hierarchy is also said to figure in the **sonority sequencing principle**.

sonority sequencing principle The idea that sequences of consonants in the **onset** of a **syllable** increase in sonority, according to the **sonority hierarchy**, as one heads towards the **nucleus** of the syllable, which is taken to be the most sonorous sound in the syllable. The principle also claims that sequences of consonants in the **coda** of a syllable decrease in sonority as one heads away from the nucleus. The idea has some validity, and works well for words such English *pleased* (/pli:zd/). But there appear to be many exceptions, and the facts are complicated by the presence of suffix consonants within a syllable (as in *pleads*), as well as the existence of **syllabic consonants**.

Southern US accent Most agree that the linguistic South in the USA is in the South-east, and that the linguistic South begins in the state of South Carolina, extending south into the states of Georgia and northern Florida, and west into the states of Virginia, Kentucky, Arkansas, Tennessee, Alabama, Mississippi and Louisiana. Quite how the vast state of Texas fits into this is unclear; Eastern Texan accents are to some extent **non-rhotic**, as in the neighbouring state of Louisiana, which all agree is Southern. Some include the state of North Carolina in the linguistic South of the USA.

SPE *The Sound Pattern of English*, a book published in 1968 by Noam **Chomsky** and Morris **Halle**. It is often seen as the founding text for **generative phonology**.

SPE phonology The model of **generative phonology** adopted in the book **SPE**, based on the combined notions of **rule** and **representation**, coupled with the idea that rules apply to **underlying representations** to yield **derived** representations. The transition from an underlying representation to a **surface** phonetic representation is known as a **derivation**, and models of phonological organisation based on this idea are known as **derivational phonologies**, as distinct from non-derivational models such as various versions of **declarative phonology**.

spectrogram A visual display of the component parts of a sound wave, made by a device known as a sound spectrograph. Spectrograms have two axes, the horizontal one showing the number of milliseconds that have elapsed in a recording, and the vertical one showing the frequencies of the **formants** of the speech sounds.

spirantisation Fricativisation: the **process** in which **stops** become **fricatives**. This has happened as a historical change in many languages. In the history of Spanish, voiced stops underwent spirantisation in **intervocalic** position. Thus, a word such as *lugar* ('place') changed over time from having the **voiced velar** stop [g] to having the voiced velar fricative [ɣ]. The same spirantisation process happened with the voiced **bilabial** stop [b], which became the voiced bilabial fricative [β], and the voiced **dental** stop [d̪], which became the voiced dental fricative [ð]. Spirantisation is one form of **lenition**.

split A term used in the phonemic tradition when describing historical change in **phoneme** systems. A phonemic split is said to have taken place when a sound which had **allophonic** status takes on **phonemic** status over time. **Nasalised** vowels used to be allophones of **oral** vowels in the history of French, occurring before **nasal stops**. But, with the **elision** of **word-final** nasal stops in the history of the language, the present-day nasalised vowel phonemes of Standard French emerged, as seen in **minimal pairs** such as [bo] *beau* ('beautiful') and [bõ] *bon* ('good').

Spoonerism A kind of speech error named after the Reverend W. A. Spooner. Examples are 'You have hissed my mystery lecture and were caught fighting a liar in the quad,' instead of 'You have missed my history lecture and were caught lighting a fire in the quad.' Spoonerisms involve the transposition of **segments**, **syllables** or words. The process is often mistakenly described in popular definitions as the transposition of letters, rather than segments. Spoonerisms are interesting for phonologists because they give us insight into syllabic **constituents**, **articulatory planning** and the **mental lexicon**. In the examples just given, not only are word-initial **onsets** transposed, but the result of the transposition in each case is a well-formed word which is stored in the mental lexicon.

spread glottis Open glottis: a **laryngeal feature** said to be present in sounds which are **aspirated**.

square brackets The brackets used in **phonetic transcription**, as for the English word *pull*: [pʰʊɫ]. They are distinct from **slanted brackets**, which are used in **phonemic transcription**, and are thus used for visual representation of **underlying representations**. In reality, books and articles on phonology frequently fail to stick consistently to the use of slanted brackets for phonemic representations and square brackets for phonetic representations, and indeed some authors often use no brackets at all.

standard A standard variety of a language is a variety which happens to have undergone the sociohistorical process of standardisation, in which fixed forms of words are established as the 'correct' pronunciations, and certain grammatical structures are also deemed to be 'correct'. Several different sociolinguistic and sociopolitical factors may lead to the **standardisation** of a language variety, including, in many cases, the translation of the Bible into that variety and the adopting of an agreed-upon spelling system. Examples of standard varieties are Standard French (as opposed to Midi French) and Castillian Spanish (as opposed to, say, Andalucian Spanish). Regional standards also exist, as in the case of Standard Jamaican English.

Standard Scottish English (SSE) An **accent** of English spoken predominantly by the educated middle classes in Scotland. Most Scots speak SSE, but many mix this with **Scots** to varying degrees. Generally speaking, the more Scots in a speaker's speech, the more Scottish they will sound, and the more working class. SSE differs from **Received Pronunciation** in many phonological respects, one of which is the presence of the **Scottish Vowel Length Rule**. Sometimes referred to as **Scottish Standard English**.

Standard Southern British English (SSBE) see **Received Pronunciation**

standardisation see **standard**

stiff vocal folds A **laryngeal feature** said to be present in **voiceless** sounds.

stimulus A term used in **Behaviourism** in conjunction with the term 'response'. Stimulus-response Behaviourism took **utterances** of speakers to be stimuli which induced a verbal response on the part of the hearer. On this view, one conceives of **phonology**, not as phonological knowledge, but as a set of verbal behavioural patterns and dispositions to behave verbally in certain ways.

The term is used quite differently by the followers of Noam **Chomsky** to refer to the ambient language (the input) to which the human child is exposed. Chomskyans adopt the **Poverty of the Stimulus argument**, claiming that the stimulus is impoverished, in that it is full of hesitations, false starts, errors and uncompleted sentences. Having assumed this, they go on to argue that a child could not acquire a language without the aid of innate linguistic knowledge. Linguists such as the British **Empiricist** linguist Geoffrey **Sampson** assume the richness of the stimulus, and argue that everything the child has to acquire is present in the stimulus. As far as phonological knowledge is concerned, Sampson's view is that all of the phonological knowledge that the child has to acquire is present in the input.

stochastic phonology Probabilistic phonology. Human beings are capable, from birth, of extracting statistical probabilities from the stream of speech. These include the probability of a given speech sound to follow another speech sound. For instance, given a complex **onset** cluster in English starting with a **stop**, the following **segment** will be one of the **approximants** /w, j, l, ɹ/; the probability of any other segment type occurring in that position is zero. The transitions between segment types are different across word boundaries from what they are within words. Because infants can extract such probabilities from the stream of speech, this helps considerably with the **bootstrapping problem**. Those who adopt stochastic approaches to the acquisition of phonology and of morphological and syntactic knowledge tend to argue for the richness of the **stimulus** to which the child is exposed. This approach stands in stark contrast to the approach of Noam **Chomsky**, who argues that the stimulus is impoverished.

stop see **degree of stricture**

strata see **stratal phonology**

stratal phonology Any model of the interaction of **phonology** and **morphology** which postulates different levels or **strata** of affixation, with specific phonological operations or **constraints** holding at specific levels of word formation. **Lexical Phonology** is an example.

strengthening see **fortition**

stress The term is often used to refer to **word stress**, synonymous with one of the senses of **accent**. However, phonologists also use the term when referring to **phrasal stress** and **sentence stress**.

stress and intonation language A language like English, which has both a **word stress** system and an **intonation** system, but which is neither a **tone language** nor a **pitch accent language**.

stress clash a situation in which two stressed **syllables** in a word are adjacent. Many languages exhibit **stress clash avoidance**. In English, when one word is derived from another by the addition of **affixes**, there is a tendency to place a **secondary stress** on the syllable which had a **primary stress** in the deriving word, as in ˌcharacter-iˈsation, where a secondary stress has been placed on the syllable which has primary stress in ˈcharacter. But where this tendency would result in a stress clash, the secondary stress is placed so as to avoid a stress clash, as in ˌJapanˈese, where the placement of the secondary stress on the syllable which has primary stress in Jaˈpan would result in a stress clash; we avoid saying Jaˌpaˈnese.

stress clash avoidance see **stress clash**

stress retraction A term sometimes used to refer to the kind of reversal one encounters in phenomena such as

Iambic Reversal. When expressions such as *East London* occur in phrases such as *East London Airport*, the prominence levels (stress levels) of *East* and *London* are switched around; the stress on *London* is said to be retracted, so that *East* becomes more prominent than *London*.

stress-timed A language is said to have stress-timed **rhythm** if the beats fall on the stressed **syllables**. It is often claimed that most varieties of English are stress-timed. This claim rests on the idea that there is a tendency for the time between the beats to be the roughly same, or **isochronous**. See **syllable-timed**.

stressed vowel A **vowel** which is stressed, as in the vowel [ɪ] in the English word *ambiguous*: [æmˈbɪgjuəs]. Stressed vowels can have either **primary** or **secondary stress**.

stricture see **degree of stricture**

structural analogy The idea that the structure of phonological **constituents** is analogous to the structure of syntactic constituents. For instance, some linguists believe that the structure of **syllables** is parallel in some serious sense with the structure of sentences, in that both are said to contain constituents, and both are said to exhibit **hierarchical structure**. The idea can be found in the work of the Danish linguist **Louis Hjelmslev** and, more recently, in **Dependency Phonology**, **Government Phonology** and **Head-Driven Phonology**.

Structuralism see **structuralist linguistics**

structuralist linguistics In a sense, all forms of linguistics are structuralist, since linguists are typically interested in structure and believe that human languages have structure. But the term 'structuralist' has been used to denote several traditions in linguistics. Firstly, the European tradition which started with **Saussure**, and continued with the **Prague School**, is often called **European Structuralism**. Central ideas here are the notions of **sign**, **markedness** and systems of **opposition**. Secondly, the kinds of linguistics practised in the United States in the 1930s to the 1950s are often referred to as **American Structuralism**. A key idea here was **distribution**; both in syntax and in phonology, it was held that one could identify the distribution of syntactic and phonological objects, and thus arrive at an analysis of a language. Scholars working within **generative linguistics** argue that there was a radical break, or 'revolution' between pre-generative American Structuralism and generative linguistics. Others claim that generative linguistics shares so many assumptions with American Structuralism that it is wise to label both generative and pre-generative American linguistics as 'structuralist'.

structuralist phonology see **structuralist linguistics**

substance-free An approach to phonological structure which is substance-free attempts to define phonological objects independently of phonetic substance. On this view, phonological objects have no **intrinsic phonetic content**. See **phonetics-free phonology** and **Hjelmslev**.

supralaryngeal Articulatory features and gestures which are supralaryngeal are articulated above the **larynx**. Articulations involving the tongue and lips are examples.

suprasegmental Concerning phonological phenomena above the level of the **segment**, such as **word stress, intonation** and **tone**.

surface form Often distinguished from **underlying representation**. The general idea, found in **derivational** theories of phonology, is that surface forms are somehow closer to the actual pronunciation of the word in question. For example, the surface form of the English word *period* is ['pʰiːɹiəd] in many varieties. This more closely represents the actual pronunciation by many speakers than a postulated underlying representation such as /piːɹiɒd/. In the latter representation, the **primary stress** is omitted on the grounds that English **word stress** is predictable. **Aspiration** is also omitted because it too is said to be predictable (i.e. **allophonic**), and the non-reduced vowel /ɒ/ is postulated as forming part of the underlying representation, because the stress assignment principles are said to reduce it, in a predictable manner, to the unstressed vowel [ə] (**schwa**).

Sweet, Henry (1845–1912) A British phonetics/phonology scholar based at Oxford University. Sweet worked on the history of English and on the transcription of English and other languages. His work contains an appeal to the distinction between **phonemic** and **phonetic** representations. It has been widely assumed that Sweet was the model for Professor Henry Higgins in George Bernard Shaw's play *Pygmalion* (which forms the basis for the film *My Fair Lady*), but the British phonetician Beverley Collins has argued persuasively that Higgins was modelled on Daniel **Jones**.

syllabic consonants **Consonants** which occupy the **nucleus** of a syllable. Transcribed with a subscript **diacritic**

under the consonant symbol. In English, the pronunciation [hæʔm̩] of the word *happen* is **bisyllabic**, the
second syllable consisting of a syllabic [m].

syllabification The **process** whereby **segments** are slotted
into syllabic positions. Principles such as **Maximal
Onset** are said to guide the syllabification of segments.

syllable A unit of phonological organisation whose
central component is a **nucleus**, which is normally a
vowel, and which may be preceded or followed by **consonants**. The most basic kind of syllable is the CV
(Consonant-Vowel) syllable (e.g. [ba]). This is the kind
of syllable attested in the **babbling** stage of child development. Some languages contain only CV syllables.
The syllable is often said to be subdivided into the
onset (any consonants preceding the nucleus) and the
rhyme (the nucleus and any consonants following
the nucleus). The rhyme is said to be further subdivided
into the nucleus and the **coda** (any consonants following the nucleus). Thus, in the English word *but* (/bʌt/),
the onset contains /b/ and the sequence /ʌt/ constitutes
the rhyme, which contains the nucleus /ʌ/ and the coda
consonant /t/. Syllables which contain no coda consonants are **open syllables,** as in the English word *bee*
(/biː/). Syllables which contain one or more coda consonants are **closed syllables,** as in the English word *but*.
Syllables which lack an onset consonant are said to
have an **empty onset,** as in the English word *eye* (/ai/).
Empty onsets are said to be involved in the process of
resyllabification, whereby a consonant which might
otherwise occupy a coda position comes to occupy a
following onset position, as in the sequence *green eye*,
syllabified as /griː.nai/ (where the full stop represents a
syllable boundary).

syllable quantity A synonym for **syllable weight**.

syllable-timed A language is said to be syllable-timed if the beats in the **rhythm** fall on each successive **syllable**, regardless of whether it is stressed or not. It is often said that French is syllable-timed. See **stress-timed**.

syllable weight A notion based on the distinction between **heavy syllables** and **light syllables**. Generally speaking, heavy syllables have more weight, or **quantity**, in the **rhyme**, in the form of more **segments**, or longer segments, than do light syllables. In many languages, a syllable containing a **long** vowel in the **nucleus** will count as heavy, whereas a syllable containing a **short** vowel will count as light. **Coda** consonants often contribute to syllable weight, so that a syllable containing a short vowel followed by a coda consonant will count as a heavy syllable. The distinction is often appealed to in analyses of **word stress** assignment. In many languages, only heavy syllables in certain positions may be stressed. For instance, in Latin, a heavy **penultimate** syllable was stressed, as in *rela:tus* (with a long vowel in the penultimate syllable) and *refectus* (with a short vowel and a coda consonant in the penultimate syllable). When **tree diagrams** are used to represent syllable structure, it is often claimed that a heavy syllable can be defined as a syllable with a branching rhyme.

synchronic Related to **synchrony**. The study of the synchronic phonology of a language is the study of its present-day phonology, rather than its **historical phonology**.

synchrony The present day, rather than the past. Opposed to **diachrony**.

syncope The **deletion** (**elision**) of a **vowel**, resulting in the loss of a **syllable**, as in the **bisyllabic** pronunciation ['fæmli] (*family*), as opposed to the **trisyllabic** pronunciation ['fæmɪli]. In English, this deletion typically affects unstressed syllables.

systematic phonemic level of representation see **representation**

systematic phonetic level of representation see **representation**

systematic phonological representation A synonym for **systematic phonemic level of representation**.

systemic differences A difference between two varieties of a language is said to be systemic if the varieties exhibit differences in the set of phonemic **oppositions** found in those varieties. For example, in **Received Pronunciation** (**RP**), there is a phonemic opposition between **short** /æ/, as in the word *ant*, and **long** /ɑː/, as in the word *aunt*. In **Standard Scottish English** (**SSE**), this opposition does not exist; pairs of words such as *ant/aunt* are **homophones**, both being pronounced [ɐnt], with a **low central vowel**, half-way between [æ] and [ɑː]. See **realisational differences** and **lexical-distributional differences**. The three-way conceptual distinction between systemic, realisational and lexical-distributional differences goes back at least as far as the work of **Trubetzkoy**, although he used different terms for each of the members of the trichotomy.

☐ T

tap see **flap**

Tapping see **Flapping**

tautosyllabic A sound is said to be tautosyllabic if it is produced in the same **syllable** as some other sound. For instance, the [ł] in the English word *full* is tautosyllabic with the preceding vowel.

teleological Goal-orientated, or purpose-orientated. Some phonologists believe that we can conceive of sound changes in the history of human languages as 'conspiring' towards specific outcomes. An example would be the various vowel **lengthening** and vowel **shortening** changes which led to the elimination of phonemic vowel **length** in **Scots** and **Standard Scottish English**. See **conspiracy**.

template Generalised phonological patterns, such as CCVC, where the 'C' stands for 'consonant' and the 'V' stands for 'vowel'. In **generative phonology**, templates are appealed to in the analysis of Arabic and in the study of reduplication patterns: see **reduplication** for examples. Also see **radical consonants**.

In the field of child phonology, templates are appealed to in the work of Marilyn **Vihman**. These are generalised patterns, such as /CVlV/, specific to the speech of an individual child. Examples of French child utterances conforming to that template are [lɛla] (*Il/Elle est là*: 'He/She is there') and [sɛla] (*C'est là:* 'It's there'). Vihman argues that **utterances** which conform to the child's templates are perceptually **salient** to the child, and that the child will select such utterances in his/her attempt at adult utterances. She also argues that infants will adapt adult utterance so that they are slotted into the templatic pattern, as in our example [lɛla], which does not conform exactly to the targeted adult forms.

tense A **feature** which has often been postulated to account for certain vowel **oppositions**, such as the oppositions /iː/ vs /ɪ/ and /uː/ vs /ʊ/ in **RP**, where the first member of the pair is said to be 'tense' and the second member '**lax**'. One definition claims that tense vowels are articulated with 'heightened subglottal pressure'. Other definitions take tense vowels, as opposed to lax vowels, to be articulated closer to the periphery of the **vowel space**, and to be typically longer than their lax counterparts. Both of these are certainly true for the RP pairs just mentioned, but the term 'tense' remains controversial. Some equate it with **Advanced Tongue Root**, while others question this equation.

tensing Any **process** in which a **segment** is said to be articulated with greater tension. The process known as 'happY tensing' in various varieties of English affects the **word-final** vowel written <-y> in words such as *happy*, yielding a tense [i], rather than a lax [ɪ]. The opposite of **laxing**.

tertiary stress see **word stress**

TH-Fronting An informal term for the uttering of **labiodental fricatives** in place of **dental** fricatives, as in the pronunciations [fɪŋ] for *thing* and [fɛvə] for *feather*. This is attested in child language acquisition and in many **non-standard** varieties of English.

TH-Stopping The pronunciation of the **dental fricatives** /θ/ and /ð/ as **stops**, often the dental stops [t̪] and [d̪]. This is attested in child language acquisition and in several varieties of English, such as **New York City English**, Indian English and Standard Jamaican English, as in pronunciations such as [t̪ɪŋ] for *thing*.

tip of the tongue The very foremost part of the tongue, often involved in **dental** articulations.

tip of the tongue phenomenon The state of affairs in which people report that a word is almost, but not quite, within reach of retrieval from the **mental lexicon;** the word is said by English speakers to be 'on the tip of my tongue'. This is relevant for phonologists, since psycholinguistic research suggests that certain phonological properties of the word in question, such as its initial **onset** consonant or its **stress** pattern, can sometimes be retrieved, even though the entire phonological form of the word cannot. This is relevant for theories of how phonological information is stored in the mind.

ToBI Tone and Break Index. ToBI is a notational system for the description of intonational patterns which originates in the work of Janet **Pierrehumbert**. The **tones** in question are intonational tones and the breaks are various kinds of **juncture**. The essence of the ToBI system is the breaking down of intonation contours into their component high and low tones. The ToBI system is used a great deal in the USA, but less among phonologists working in the British tradition.

token see **type**

token frequency see **frequency of occurrence**

Tomasello, Michael A child syntax specialist who rejects the **Chomskyan** notion of innate linguistic knowledge. In its place, he argues for a **constructivist** approach to child language acquisition, emphasising the child's social interaction with other human beings.

Although his work is in the acquisition of syntax, the general approach carries over into the acquisition of phonology.

Tone Bearing Unit (TBU) In **tone languages**, the segmental material to which a **tone** is attached. This is usually a **vowel**, as in the case of vowels in the utterance [míbú] ('my stone') in the Kwa language Twi. **Consonants** can also act as TBUs.

tone see **tone language**. The term 'tone' is used by some phonologists, in describing non-tone languages, to refer to the **pitch** changes that occur on the **nuclear syllable** (also known as the nucleus, or the **tonic syllable**) in an **intonation group**. Examples of tones referred to in the description of English intonation are the falling tone, the rising tone, the fall-rise and the rise-fall. Consider the question 'Has Mary been seeing Bill?' The response 'No!' with a rise-fall tone, conveys certainty, and the response 'No', with a fall-rise tone, conveys hesitation or doubt. The rise tone in English is associated with questioning, as in 'Has Mary been seeing Bill?'

tone group see **intonation group**

tone language A language in which **pitch** differences function to differentiate words. Tones are often subdivided into level tones and contour tones. Typical level tones are **high** vs **mid** vs **low** tones. High tones have a higher relative pitch than mid tones, which in turn have a relatively higher pitch than low tones. High tones are often transcribed using the acute accent, as in the word kó, which means 'build' in the African language Yoruba. Low tones are often transcribed using the grave accent, as in the Yoruba word kò, which means 'refuse'. Mid tones are often transcribed with no marker, as in the Yoruba word ko, which means 'sing', though some writers use a level **diacritic** for mid tones, so that 'sing' in Yoruba would be transcribed as kō. The segmental material in these three Yoruba words is the same; they differ only with respect to tone, which is a **suprasegmental** property. Non-tone languages, such as English, do not exhibit this phenomenon. Contour tones include rising tones and falling tones. Rising tones are often transcribed using a wedge diacritic, as in the Thai word nǎ, which means 'thick'. Falling tones are often transcribed with a circumflex, as in the Thai word nâ, which means 'face'. Tone languages can be found in many parts of the world, including Africa, Asia and South America.

tongue root That part of the tongue which lies behind the **back of the tongue,** opposite the back wall of the **pharynx**.

tonic see **tonic syllable**

tonic placement The placement of the **tonic** in an **intonation group**.

tonic syllable The **syllable** in an **intonation group** on which the **pitch** changes. In the English sentence *John went to the pub*, the 'neutral' (least **marked**) intonation has *pub* as the tonic syllable. It is often argued that the basic rule for the placement of the tonic syllable in English is on the **last lexical item** in a clause, as is the case here.

tonic vowel A vowel which receives primary **word stress**, as in the **antepenultimate** syllable of the Spanish word *bueno* ('good'). Not to be confused with the term 'tonic' used in studies of **intonation**.

tonogenesis The historical **process** in which a non-tone language becomes a **tone language**. There is a natural affinity between, on the one hand, **voiceless obstruents** and **high** tones, and, on the other, **voiced** obstruents and **low** tones. High tones and voiceless obstruents are characterised by stiff **vocal cords**, whereas low tones and voiced obstruents are characterised by slack vocal cords. Tonal contrasts can often be reconstructed as voicing contrasts. For example, a sequence of a voiced obstruent and a following vowel can develop into a voiced obstruent and a vowel with a low tone.

transduction see **realisation**

transformation A term used in the earlier stages of **generative linguistics**. Transformational **rules** were postulated which applied to a **representation** to yield a derived representation, by means of inserting, deleting or transposing elements of syntactic structure. In **SPE** phonology, two of the rules postulated for many varieties of English were Nasal Assimilation and Voiced Velar Deletion. In words of the sort *sing* and *bring*, they applied as follows: Underlying Representation: /sɪng/; Nasal Assimilation: /sɪŋg/; Voiced Velar Deletion: /sɪŋ/. The second and third of these are derived representation. In phonological frameworks which are **derivational**, it is possible to formulate certain phonological rules as transformations. For instance, in Lithuanian, there is a **process** of **metathesis** under which a **fricative** + **stop** sequence is switched around when such a sequence occurs before a consonant, as in /dresk/ + /kite/, which 'becomes' [drekskite].

This process can be construed as a transformational rule which transposes two elements.

transparent vowel see **neutral vowel**

tree diagram A type of visual representation of a structure, used in both syntax and phonology. Tree diagrams take the same form as the family trees used in genealogy; they consist of a central **node** which branches on to other nodes, which themselves have branches. They are used to represent the idea of **constituents**, both in syntax and phonology. In phonology, tree diagrams have been used to represent the structure of **syllables** and **feet**. They have also been used in work on **feature geometry**.

trill A sound made with a rapid series of closures and openings, as in the **alveolar** trill [r], where the **blade** of the tongue closes against the **alveolar ridge**, then opens, then closes again and so on, in quick succession. Trills can be made at two other points of articulation. **Bilabial** trills, transcribed as [B], involve rapid closures and openings between the lips. **Uvular** trills, transcribed as [R], involve the same kind of articulation, but with the **back of the tongue** as the **active articulator** and the **uvula** as the **passive articulator**.

trisyllabic Containing three **syllables**. The English words *cinema*, *horizon* and *kangaroo* are all trisyllabic.

Trisyllabic Laxing Also known as Trisyllabic Shortening, this was a change that took place in the history of English whose effect can be seen in certain **alternations** in present-day English. In **bisyllabic** words which contained a stressed long (**tense**) vowel, the addition of a suffix meant that the word had three or more syllables, and the vowel in question then underwent laxing/shortening. An examples of the residue of this change in present-day English is the pair *serene/serenity*, where bisyllabic *serene* has the long stressed vowel [iː], but *serenity* has the **short/lax** vowel [ɛ].

trochaic see **rhythm**

trochaic bias hypothesis The claim that infants are predisposed towards **trochaic**, rather than **iambic**, **metrical feet**.

trochee see **rhythm**

Trubetzkoy, Nikolaj (1890–1938) A Russian prince who fled Russia at the time of the Russian Revolution. Trubetzkoy's name is widely associated with the **Prague School** (although he actually spent most of his career in Vienna). He was known for his collaboration with Roman **Jakobson**. Trubetzkoy insisted on a distinction between **phonetics** and **phonology**, but rejected a **mentalistic** (psychological, sometimes termed '**cognitive**') interpretation of phonology. He was interested in systems of **opposition** between **phonemes**. Central ideas in Trubetzkoy's work are the identification of different kinds of phonological opposition (bilateral, multilateral, proportional, isolated, privative, gradual and equipollent oppositions). He also developed the notion of the **neutralisation** of phonological oppositions. Connected with this is the appeal to **markedness** in phonological oppositions.

true geminate see **geminate**

Tyneside English The variety of English spoken in the area around the River Tyne in the North-East of England. Also known as **Geordie**.

type/token The type/token distinction goes back to the work of the American philosopher C. S. **Peirce** (1839–1914) and has been adopted in most areas of linguistics. Tokens are specific objects or events at a particular point in space and time, such as the utterance of a **voiceless aspirated alveolar stop** ([t]) by a specific speaker at a specific point in time. Types are said to be more **abstract** than this; it may be claimed that a large set of utterances of voiceless alveolar stops are tokens of the type, or kind, 'voiceless alveolar stop'. Types may be viewed as categories, and many believe that human perception relies heavily on classifying objects and events into categories. Tokens of a type are said to 'count as the same thing', so that, when one hears a given [t], it counts as an occurrence of 'the same thing' as another, slightly different, [t], uttered on another occasion.

type frequency see **frequency of occurrence**

typological Relating to **typology**. The term is used in syntax, morphology and phonology. An example of a postulated typological difference in phonology is the three-way distinction between **stress and intonation languages**, **tone languages** and **pitch accent languages**.

typology The study of different linguistic types. In phonology, the term can subsume the study of different **word stress** systems, the study of different **vowel harmony** systems or the study of **natural classes**.

U

umlaut A kind of **metaphony** in which a **vowel** (normally in a **root**) **assimilates** to another vowel (normally in a suffix), even though the two vowels are not adjacent to each other. An example is the historical **process** of i-umlaut in German, in which the **back** vowels [u], [o] and [ɔ] in a root fronted to [y], [ø] and [œ] respectively when the plural suffix [-i] was added. For instance, in present-day German, the singular noun *Sohn* ('son') has a **high mid**, back vowel [o] in the root, but the plural *Söhne* has the umlauted version of that vowel: [ø], which is high mid and **front**. Historically, this word, like many others, had a plural suffix consisting of the high front vowel [i]. For some scholars, umlaut is a process in which a vowel in a root assimilates to a vowel in a suffix, while **vowel harmony** is a process in which a vowel in a suffix assimilates to one or more vowels in a root.

unaspirated **Voiceless stops** which are unaspirated can be defined as having no delay in **Voice Onset Time**; the **voicing** for a following vowel begins at the point at which the stop closure is released, as in the French word *pain* ('bread'): [pɛ̃]. These are distinct from the voiceless **aspirated** stops of most varieties of English, as in the word *pad*: [pʰæd].

underlying representation A level of **representation** postulated in theories which are **derivational** in nature. In **rule**-based derivational theories such as **SPE, morphophonological alternations** were dealt with by postulating a single underlying representation from which the **surface forms** could be derived. For alternants such as Hungarian [kut] ('well') and [kudban] ('in the well'), a single underlying representation /kut/ is postulated, from which the surface form [kud] is derived via a **process** of voicing assimilation.

underspecification An **underlying representation** is said to be underspecified if any of its **features** are not present, or are not assigned a value. In the Bantu language Lumasaaba, there is a prefix which attaches only to nouns beginning with a consonant. The realisations of the prefix are [zim], [zin], [ziɲ] and [ziŋ], as in [zimbati] ('knives'), [zindaha] ('wings'), [ziɲɟeɟele] ('buds') and [ziŋgunija] ('bags'). The place of articulation of the **nasal** at the end of the prefix is entirely predictable; it will have the same **place of articulation** as the following consonant, because of **nasal assimilation**. Phonologists who argue that underlying representations should contain only arbitrary, non-predictable features postulate a **nasal stop** at the end of the prefix which is underspecified; it is stripped of all place of articulation feature values. Phonologists such as Joan **Bybee**, who adopt **exemplar theory**, argue against this approach; they claim that words are stored in the mind in full phonetic detail, including entirely predictable information.

Universal Grammar (UG) A term associated with the work of Noam **Chomsky**. It is used as a name for a postulated innate **module** of mind said to contain specifically linguistic knowledge. Chomsky now uses the expression only for the theory of this postulated module, preferring the term 'the human language faculty' for that module. But many of his followers continue to use the term for both the theory and its object. The existence of innate linguistic knowledge is hotly disputed by many scholars.

universals The term is used in at least two different senses. For the followers of Noam **Chomsky**, who believe in the existence of **Universal Grammar**, linguistic universals are universal principles, given by a supposedly innate language **module**, which operate in all human languages. This is a strong sense of the term, since the universal principles postulated are absolute. An example of an absolute syntactic universal would be the claim that all human languages exhibit **recursion**. An example of a phonological universal would be the statement that all languages have both consonants and vowels. For other linguists, talk of universals is talk of tendencies in human languages, such as the tendency for vowels to **nasalise** when adjacent to a **nasal stop**. This is a weaker sense of the term. It is conceptually possible to allow that there are absolute universals while denying that they are given by Universal Grammar. **Implicational universals** take the following form: if a given language has property X, then it will also have property Y. An example would be: if a given language has voiced **obstruents**, then it will also have **voiceless** obstruents. See **Jakobson**.

unmarked see **markedness**

unrounded Lacking lip-rounding. **Front** vowels are typically unrounded, as in the vowels [i] and [e], but there are front rounded vowels too, as in the case of the French vowels [y], [ø] and [œ], found in the words *lune* ('moon'), *peu* ('little') and *sœur* ('sister').

unstressed Bearing neither **primary stress** nor secondary **stress**. In the English word *happen*, the final syllable is unstressed, while the **penultimate** syllable has primary stress. Unstressed syllables often have **reduced vowels**.

usage-based phonology An approach to phonology, associated with the work of Joan **Bybee,** which stresses that **performance** (actual usage in specific contexts of **utterance**) is as central to our understanding of phonological phenomena as **competence.** A key notion in usage-based phonology is **frequency of occurrence.**

utterance A term sometimes used in its ordinary, everyday sense to mean a stretch of uninterrupted speech made by a speaker. It has been used more technically in the literature in **generative linguistics** when a distinction is made between **sentences** and utterances, with the former seen as units of **competence** generated by a grammar, and the latter as units of **performance** produced by a speaker. However, the generative literature is inconsistent in its usage of this distinction. In discussion of the **prosodic hierarchy,** the utterance is often postulated as the largest unit in the hierarchy.

uvula The part of the **soft palate** which can be seen dangling down at the back of the mouth.

uvular Sounds which have the **back of the tongue** as the **active articulator** and the **uvula** as the **passive articulator** are uvular. **Stops, fricatives** and **approximants** can all be produced in this way. An example of a voiced uvular fricative is the 'r' sound produced in Northern French, as in the word *rat* ('rat'), pronounced [ʁɐ].

| V |

V Stands for **vowel.** For instance, when phonologists speak of **CV syllables,** they mean syllables consisting simply of an **onset consonant** and a vowel in the **nucleus** position.

van der Hulst, Harry A Dutch phonologist who has worked on, among other things, **vowel harmony** systems and **word stress** systems. He has developed a descriptive famework for phonological **representations** known as **Head-Driven Phonology**. See **structural analogy**.

variegated babbling see **babbling**

velar **A place of articulation.** Velar sounds are characterised by an articulation between the **back of the tongue** and the **velum**.

velar softening see **palatalisation**

velaric airstream mechanism see **airstream mechanisms**

velarisation A **secondary articulation** made by the **back of the tongue** and the **velum**. It is often said that the 'dark l' in many accents of English has a **primary articulation** which is **alveolar** and a secondary articulation which is velar. This velarised [l] is transcribed with a **diacritic** which runs through the phonetic symbol for the consonant, thus: [nʌɫ] (null).

velarised Articulated with a **secondary articulation** of **velarisation**.

velic Relating to the **velum**. Used to refer to **velic closure**, in which the velum is raised, preventing air from flowing through the **nasal cavity**, and **velic opening** (or lowering) in which the velum is lowered and air may flow through the nasal cavity.

velic closure see **velic**

velic opening see **velic**

velum The **soft palate**: the soft part of the palate, located behind the **hard palate**.

verlan see **language games**

Vihman, Marilyn A specialist in child phonology who has carried out extensive empirical investigation with infants. Vihman is a **constructivist** who opposes the **Chomskyan** conception of child linguistic development. See **template**.

vocal cords Two strips of tissue located in the **larynx**, which may vibrate, leading to **voicing**. During the production of **voiceless** sounds, the vocal cords are said to be **slack**, whereas they are said to be **stiff** during the production of voiced sounds. Note that the term is not spelled 'vocal chords'.

vocal folds A synonym for the **vocal cords**.

vocal play A stage in the first year of life, which starts before the **babbling** period. During this period, the child seems to be experimenting with its vocal apparatus. The sounds produced are not syllabic in nature, unlike the **CV syllables** of the babbling period. They include a range of relatively 'exotic' sounds such as **clicks** and **bilabial** and **uvular trills**.

vocal tract The three **resonance chambers** taken together: the **oral cavity**, the **nasal cavity** and the **pharynx**.

Voice Onset Time (VOT) When one produces a **stop** consonant in which the **vocal cords** are not vibrating, and then follows this with a vowel sound, there may be a delay in the onset of **voicing** in the vowel. When this happens, we say that the stop in question is **aspirated**, as in the English word *pad*: [pʰæd]. If there is no such delay in VOT, we say that the stop is **unaspirated**, as in the French word *pain* ('bread'): [pɛ̃].

voiced A term for speech sounds which are produced with **voicing**. Many phonologists have pointed out that the voiced/**voiceless** dichotomy alone is insufficient to distinguish between the full range of **laryngeal** contrasts in human languages. One needs, at least, to distinguish between the following: (a) fully voiced **stops**, in which the **vocal cords** are vibrating prior to the release of the stop closure, as in the French word *bain* ('bath'): [bɛ̃]; (b) voiceless **unaspirated** stops, as in the French word *pain* ('bread'): [pɛ̃]; (c) voiceless **aspirated** stops, as in the English word *pad*: [pʰæd]. It has been pointed out that, although English spelling conventions represent words such as *bed* with the <b> **grapheme**, the sound in question is not, in fact, a fully voiced stop, but an unaspirated voiceless stop, unlike the stop at the beginning of the French word *bain*. The contrast among French stops is thus a contrast between fully voiced and voiceless unaspirated stops, while the contrast in most varieties of English is between voiceless aspirated and voiceless unaspirated stops. Languages such as Thai have a three-way **phonemic** contrast between fully voiced, voiceless unaspirated and voiceless aspirated stops, as in the words [bàː] ('shoulder'), [pàː] ('forest') and [pʰàː] ('split').

voiceless Speech sounds are said to be voiceless if the **vocal cords** are not vibrating during their production. Example of voiceless sounds are the voiceless unaspirated stops [p], [t] and [k] in the English words *spilt*, *still* and *skin*, and the voiceless **fricatives** [f] and [s] in the English words *sin* and *fin*.

voicing The vibration of the **vocal cords**. Fully **voiced** sounds are produced with vibration of the vocal cords during the articulation of the sound, as in the [v] in the word *heavy*. **Word-initial stops** are fully voiced if the vocal cords are vibrating prior to the release of the stop closure, as in the French word bain ('bath'): [bɛ̃:].

voicing assimilation see **assimilation**

vowel Any sound which occupies the **nucleus** of a **syllable** and is produced with a stricture of **open approximation**. See **degree of stricture**.

vowel fronting Any **process** in which one or more **vowels** is produced further forward in the **vowel space** than it previously was. The front **rounded** vowels [y], [ø] and [œ] in contemporary Standard French all resulted from the historical fronting of the back vowels [u], [o] and [ɔ]. See also **umlaut**.

vowel harmony A kind of **metaphony** in which all the **vowels** in a word must share one or more properties (but see **opaque vowels** and **neutral vowels**), as in Finnish [tyhmæ] 'stupid' vs [tuhmɑ] 'naughty', where the first word has vowels which share the property of frontness (palatality) and the vowels in the second word all lack that property. Such languages tend to have two sets of vowels, one possessing the harmonic property, the other lacking it. Vowel harmony often spreads from **roots** to **affixes**, as in Hungarian [by:n-tøl] 'crime', where the ablative suffix undergoes

palatal harmony and thus contains a **front** vowel, unlike [mokuʃ-tol] 'squirrel', where the ablative suffix has a **back** vowel. Other properties which feature in vowel harmony include the following: (a) **labiality (roundedness)**, as in Turkish [gyl] 'rose' (nominative), [gyl-y] 'rose' (possessive) as distinct from [is] 'footprint' (nominative), [iz-i] 'footprint' (possessive); (b) lowness, as in Kikuyu, which has a suffix which takes the form [ɪr] (with a high vowel) or [er] (with a lowered vowel), determined by the height of the first vowel of the **stem**: [rut-ɪr-a] 'work for', [ror-er-a] 'look at'; (c) **Advanced Tongue Root** (ATR), as in Tangale [tug-o] 'pounding', [wʊd-ɔ] 'farming'; (d) **Retracted Tongue Root** (RTR), as in Yoruba [epo] 'oil', [ɛkɔ] 'pap'. There is often debate as to whether a given system exhibits ATR or RTR harmony. Some languages have harmony for more than one property. For instance, the Khirgiz infinitive forms [bil] 'know', [kyl] 'laugh', [kɨl] 'do' and [bol] 'be' take different forms of the past definite suffix: [bil-di], [kyl-dy], [kɨl-dɨ] and [bol-du], showing both palatal and **labial** harmony. Some languages with vowel harmony have words exhibiting **disharmony**, involving **neutral vowels** and/or **opaque vowels**. There are languages in which harmony may spread from certain affix vowels into the root: see **dominant/recessive harmony**. Vowel harmony often has no effect on intervening consonants, but there are cases where it does.

vowel quality The acoustic impression given by the production a given **vowel** type. This is difficult to pin down precisely, because there is a continuum as one moves from one vowel sound to another; there are no sharp boundaries between, say, [i], [e] and [ɛ]. None the less, it is possible for humans to identify prototypical [i]-type, [e]-type and [ɛ]-type qualities, just as we can identify prototypical examples of colours such as green and blue, even though there are colours which are intermediate between the two.

vowel raising Any **process** in which one or more **vowels** is produced higher in the **vowel space** than it previously was. In Standard French, the vowel [u] results from the historical raising of an [o] vowel, as in the transition from *trover* ('to find') to *trouver*, pronounced [tʁuve].

vowel reduction see **reduction**

vowel retraction Any **process** in which one or more **vowels** is produced further back in the **vowel space** than it previously was. In present-day **Received Pronunciation**, the back vowel [ɑ:] in words such as *class* and *grass* results from the historical retraction of front [æ:]. Also known as vowel **backing**.

vowel shift A **process** in which the **realisation** of a vowel **phoneme** encroaches on the articulatory and perceptual space of another vowel phoneme, resulting in a change in the realisation of the other vowel phoneme, apparently to 'avoid' a phonemic **merger**. In London English, the phoneme /aɪ/ is often realised as [ɑɪ] or [ɔɪ], as in *buy* pronounced [bɔɪ]. These realisations encroach upon the space of the phoneme /ɔɪ/, which may be said to 'take evasive action', and is often pronounced [oɪ], as in [boɪ] (*boy*), thus avoiding a phonemic merger and sustaining *buy/boy* as a **minimal pair**, rather than as **homophones**. The idea of 'taking evasive action' can be conveyed via the notion of 'push chain', in which one vowel phoneme can be thought of as 'pushing' an adjacent vowel into another, nearby, part of the **vowel space**. Equally, one can conceive of vowel shifts as **'pull chains'** (**drag chains**), in which one vowel phoneme 'vacates' a part of the vowel space, dragging an adjacent vowel phoneme into the vacated space. See **Great Vowel Shift** and **Northern Cities Vowel Shift**.

vowel space The space in the **oral cavity** in which **vowels** can be produced.

vowel system see **Phonemic Principle**

vowel triangle see **Dispersion Theory**

Vulgar Latin The Latin spoken at the height of the Roman Empire by ordinary working people, soldiers and merchants. It is distinct from **Classical Latin** and is the historical source of the present-day **Romance languages**.

weakening A synonym for **lenition**. See also **reduction**.

weight see **syllable weight**

well-formed A syntactic sequence in a given language is said to be well-formed if it conforms to the grammatical rules of the language. Thus *The man kicked the dog* is well-formed in English, but *Kicked dog man the the* is not. In phonology, the notion can be applied to phonological sequences. The **word-initial** sequences /kl/, /kw/, /kr/ and /kj/ are all well-formed in most varieties of English, as in the words *clown*, *queen*, *cry* and (arguably) *cure*. But word-initial sequences such as /kn/ and /ks/ are ill-formed.

Wells, J. C. A British phonetics/phonology specialist based at University College London, perhaps best known for his three-volume work *Accents of English*, published in 1982. This book is a systematic description of the pronunciation of a large number of varieties of English around the world, and is still frequently referred to today.

word boundary The boundary between two words, as in the boundary between *far* and *away* in the phrase *far away*. Word boundaries can play a role in phonological **processes**, as in the case of **Linking 'r'** in **non-rhotic** varieties of English, where a **word-final** underlying /r/ is realised if the following word begins with a vowel, as in the phrase *far away*.

Some sequences of two words are said to form a 'closer' link to each other than others, and this closeness is believed to play a role in the triggering or non-triggering of certain phonological processes. In the case of obligatory **Liaison** in French, the underlying /z/ in words such as *mes* (the plural form for 'my') is realised if the following word begins with a vowel, as in *mes amis*: [mezami]. Similarly, the plural suffix /z/ is realised in phrases such as *amis américains* ('American friends'): [amizameʁikɛ̃]. But the plural /z/ of *amis* is not realised in the expression *Mes amis arrivent* ('My friends are coming'): [mezamiaʁiv]. It is claimed that the link between *mes* and *amis* is closer than the link between *amis* and *arrivent*. It is this 'closer link' that is said to trigger the Liaison process. There is disagreement as to whether syntactic structure directly influences phonological processes, or whether the influence is indirect, mediated by phonological units such as the **phonological phrase**.

word-final Occurring at the end of a word. The **stop** /d/ is word-final in the word *bad*.

Word-Final Devoicing A **process** whereby **voiced obstruents** become **voiceless** when in **word-final** position. The Polish root /trud/ ('labour') is pronounced as [trut], since the final /d/ undergoes **devoicing**, but if the final obstruent in the root is not word-final, no devoicing occurs, as in [trudi], the plural form of the noun.

word-initial Occurring at the beginning of a word. The **stop** /b/ is word-initial in the word *bad*.

word-medial Occurring in the middle of a word. The **stop** /p/ is word-medial in the word *happen*: ['hæpən]. The term is rather vague and unsatisfactory, since it can be used to denote segments which occur in a wide variety of syllabic and metrical contexts.

word phonology see **Lexical Phonology**

word stress Whatever language we study, we will find that not all of the **syllables** in a word will have the same degree of perceptual **salience** (prominence); some will be more prominent/salient that others, as in the English word *father*, where the **penultimate** syllable is more prominent than the final syllable. This prominence/salience is known as word stress, sometimes referred to simply as stress. It can be created via any or all of the following: greater loudness, greater **segmental** or syllabic **length**, or greater **pitch** movement. Different languages harness different combinations of these in their word stress systems. In English, it is mostly pitch movement and **duration** which convey word stress. In Japanese, it is pitch movement alone (see **pitch accent**

languages). Some languages have a very simple word stress assignment system; a given syllable in the word is the one that will be stressed, such as the last syllable in the case of Standard French. Others have arbitrary patterns of stress in words, in which the stress may appear on any of the syllables of a **root**, as in Modern Greek. Yet others exhibit **rule-governed** word stress assignment. An example is Malay, where the rule is as follows: place a **primary stress** on the penultimate syllable of the word and then place a **secondary stress** on the initial syllable of the word, and each alternate syllable thereafter, subject to **stress clash avoidance**, as in the word [ˌsilatuˈrahim], where a primary stress falls on the penultimate syllable, and a secondary stress on the initial syllable. The third syllable from the beginning of the word does not take a secondary stress since this would result in a **stress clash**. Some phonologists postulate, in addition to primary stress and secondary stress, a level or **tertiary stress**, as in the English word *survey*. It is agreed that words such as this have primary stress on the penultimate syllable. Those who postulate tertiary stress on the final syllable do so because it has a vowel which does not exhibit **reduction** to **schwa** (compare the word *woman*, with primary stress on the penultimate syllable and a schwa in the final syllable. Stress is sometimes referred to as **accent** and stressed syllables are said to be accentuated.

| Y |

yers The name for a set of **abstract** underlying vowels postulated by **generative phonologists** to account for certain **morpho-phonological alternations** in the Slavic languages. In Polish, some instances of phonetic [ɛ] **alternate** with **zero**, as in [pɔsɛł] vs [pɔsła], the nominative singular and genitive singular of the word for 'envoy', where we can see [ɛ] in the nominative form, but no [ɛ] in the genitive form. These alternations are distinct from pairs such as [fɔtɛl] vs [fɔtɛla], the nominative singular and genitive singular forms of the word meaning 'armchair', where the [ɛ] does not alternate with zero. The argument is that the [ɛ]s which alternate with zero must be derived from an **underlying representation** other than /ɛ/. That underlying representation is said to be a yer, a non-**ATR** high vowel, represented as /ɨ/, which may be realised as [ɛ], or as zero. This kind of analysis is an example of **absolute neutralisation,** since there is no phonetic [ɨ] in Polish which would provide phonetic evidence for the existence of underlying /ɨ/.

yod A term used to refer to the **palatal glide** [j], often transcribed as [y] by American phonologists.

Yod Dropping A term used to refer to the non-pronunciation of **yod** in certain **accents** of English. In many varieties of American English, there is Yod Dropping in words such as *new* and *tune*, pronounced [nu:] and [tʰu:n]. Yod Dropping only applies where the yod would have been preceded by a **coronal** consonant, and thus fails to apply in words such as *cure*, pronounced [kʰjʊɹ], and *pure*, pronounced [pʰjʊɹ].

Z

zero A term often used to describe **alternations** in which a sound is **elided.** In Standard French, **schwa** is said to alternate with zero, as in the various ways of pronouncing sequences such as *Je te le redemande* ('I'm asking you this again'), where the schwa vowels in *Je,* *te le*, *re-* and *de* may be elided, subject to the **constraint** known as **la loi des trois consonnes**. An example is [ʃtələʁədmɑ̃d], where the schwas in *Je* and *de* have been elided, but not the schwas of *te*, *le* or *re-*. Many phonologists postulate an **underlying** schwa in words such as *Je*, which is said to have a zero **realisation** when it is elided.

Sources

Many of the examples come from what I know of varieties of English and French. I also know a little about Malay and Spanish, so I have used examples from those languages too. For examples from these and other languages, I have relied on the following primary and secondary sources.

Anderson, J. M. and C. J. Ewen (1987) *Principles of Dependency Phonology*, Cambridge: Cambridge University Press.

Carr, P. (1993) *Phonology*, Basingstoke: Macmillan.

Carr, P. (1999) *English Phonetics and Phonology*, Oxford: Blackwell.

Charette, M. (1991) *Conditions on Phonological Government*, Cambridge: Cambridge University Press.

Dell, F. (1980) *Generative Phonology and French Phonology*, Cambridge: Cambridge University Press. English translation of Dell (1973) *Les Règles et les sons: Introduction à la phonologie générative*, Paris: Hermann.

Durand, J. (1990) *Generative and Non-linear Phonology*, London: Longman.

Fox, J. and R. Wood (1968) *A Concise History of the French Language*, Oxford: Blackwell.

Giegerich, H. (1992) *English Phonology*, Cambridge: Cambridge University Press.

Hannahs, S. J. (1995) *Prosodic Structure and French Morphophonology*, Tübingen: Niemeyer.

Harris, J. (1994) *English Sound Structure*, Oxford: Blackwell.

Hock, H. H. (1991) *Principles of Historical Linguistics*, Berlin: Mouton de Gruyter.

Hyman, L. (1975) *Phonology: Theory and Analysis*, New York: Holt, Rinehart & Winston.

Kager, R. (1999) *Optimality Theory*, Cambridge: Cambridge University Press.

Kassin, T. A. (2000) *The Phonological Word in Standard Malay*. Unpublished PhD thesis, Newcastle University, UK.

Kenstowicz, M. (1994) *Phonology in Generative Grammar*, Oxford: Blackwell.

Lass, R. (1984) *Phonology*, Cambridge: Cambridge University Press.

Ohala, J. J. (1989) 'Sound change is drawn from a pool of synchronic variation,' in L. E. Breivik and E. H. Jahr (eds), *Language Change: Contributions to the Study of its Causes*, Berlin: Mouton de Gruyter, pp. 173–98.

Roca, I. and W. Johnson (1999) A *Course in Phonology*, Oxford: Blackwell.

Silverman, D. (2006) *A Critical Introduction to Phonology*, New York: Continuum.

Spencer, A. (1996) *Phonology*, Oxford: Blackwell.

Wells, J. C. (1982) *Accents of English*, vols 1–3, Cambridge: Cambridge University Press.

In giving brief details of various schools and scholars in the history of phonology, I have relied heavily on Stephen R. Anderson's excellent 1985 book, *Phonology in the Twentieth Century* (Chicago: University of Chicago Press). I hope to be forgiven for the extremely simplified thumbnail sketches I have offered of these schools and scholars.

I also hope that no factual errors have crept into those sketches. I have also had recourse to *Key Thinkers in Linguistics and the Philosophy of Language*, edited by Siobhan Chapman and Chris Routledge, and published in 2005 by Edinburgh University Press.

Bibliography

(a) Textbook introductions

The beginning student should follow an introductory course in phonology, preferably using a textbook which contains exercises. Of the textbooks which appear in the sources section, I recommend Spencer (1996). C. Gussenhoven and H. Jacob's (2005) *Understanding Phonology*, published by Arnold, is a useful book, as is M. Davenport and S. J. Hannahs (1998) *Introducing Phonetics and Phonology*, also published by Arnold. Carr (1993), cited above, is slightly out of date (soon to be updated), but has useful exercises. The textbooks cited above by Roca and Johnson, and by Kenstowicz, are both very good but are rather long. B. Collins and I. Mees (2003) *Practical Phonetics and Phonology*, published by Routledge, is, as the title suggests, practical in its aims, rather than being an introduction to phonological theory as such, but it is a unique and most useful book, with an excellent accompanying CD.

For students looking for an introduction to specifically English phonetics and phonology, Giegerich (1992), cited above, is a very good book but has no exercises. For an elementary introduction to English phonetics and phonology, I suggest either Carr (1999), cited above, or April McMahon's (2002) *An Introduction to English Phonology*, published by Edinburgh University Press. The

Collins and Mees book cited above is also useful for coverage of varieties of English. Mehmet Yavaş's (2006) *Applied English Phonology*, published by Blackwell, is also useful. Students should also consult the late Larry Trask's (1996) *A Dictionary of Phonetics and Phonology*, published by Routledge, which is admirable in its coverage. Students should be aware, however, that I have reservations about some of Trask's definitions (which often lack exemplification); because of this, the student will find that my definition of central terms, such as 'phoneme' differ substantially from his.

(b) Primary source material

For students wishing to consult primary source material, the following is a very partial list of books and articles which have made an impact on various parts of the field.

Anderson, J. M. and C. J. Ewen (1987) *Principles of Dependency Phonology*, Cambridge: Cambridge University Press.

Anderson, S. R. (1983) *Phonology in the Twentieth Century*, Chicago, IL: Chicago University Press.

Archangeli, D. (1988) 'Aspects of underspecification theory,' *Phonology* 5: 183–208.

Baudouin de Courtenay, J. (1972) *Selected Writings of Baudouin de Courtenay*, edited by E. Stankiewicz, Bloomington, IN: Indiana University Press.

Bloomfield, L. (1926) 'A set of postulates for the study of language,' Language 2: 153–64. Reprinted in Joos, M. (ed.) (1957), *Readings in Linguistics*, vol. 1, Washington: American Council of Learned Societies, 329–48.

Bromberger, S. and M. Halle (1989) 'Why phonology is different,' *Linguistic Inquiry* 20: 51–70.

Bybee, J. (2001) *Phonology and Language Use*, Cambridge: Cambridge University Press.

Chomsky, N. and M. Halle (1968) *The Sound Pattern of English*, New York: Harper & Row.

Clements, G. N. (1985) 'The geometry of phonological features,' *Phonology Yearbook* 2: 225–53.

Donegan, P. and D. Stampe (1979) 'The study of Natural Phonology,' in D. Dinnsen (ed.), *Current Approaches to Phonological Theory*, Bloomington, IN: Indiana University Press, 126–73.

Firth, J. R. (1934) 'The word "Phoneme",' *Le Maître phonétique* 46: 44–6.

Jones, D. (1950) *The Phoneme: its Nature and Use*, Cambridge: Heffer.

Goldsmith, J. (1979) *Autosegmental Phonology*, New York: Garland.

Hale, M. and C. Reiss (2000) 'Substance abuse and dys-functionalism: current trends in phonology,' *Linguistic Inquiry* 31: 157–69.

Halle, M. and J. R. Vergnaud (1987) *An Essay on Stress*, Cambridge, MA: MIT Press.

Hayes, B. (1982) 'Extrametricality and English stress,' *Linguistic Inquiry* 13: 227–76.

Hyman, L. (1970) 'How concrete is phonology?,' *Language* 46: 58–76.

Jakobson, R. (1962) *Selected Writings*, vol. 1, The Hague: Mouton.

Jakobson, R. (1971) *Selected Writings*, vol. 2, The Hague: Mouton.

Johnson, K. (1997) 'Speech perception without speaker normalization,' in K. Johnson and J. W. Mullenix (eds), *Talker Variability in Speech Processing*, San Diego: Academic, 145–65.

Kiparsky, P. (1968) 'How abstract is Phonology?,' reprinted in P. Kiparsky (1982) *Explanation in Phonology*, Dordrecht: Foris.

Kiparsky, P. (1982) 'From cyclic to lexical phonology,' in H. van der Hulst and N. Smith (eds), *The Structure of Phonological Representations* (2 vols), Dordrecht: Foris.

Labov, W. (1966) *The Social Stratification of English in New York City*, Washington, DC: Center for Applied Linguistics.

Liberman, M. Y. and A. Prince (1977) 'On stress and linguistic rhythm,' *Linguistic Inquiry* 8: 249–336.

McCarthy, J. and A. Prince (1995) 'Prosodic morphology,' in J. Goldsmith (ed.), *The Handbook of Phonological Theory*, Oxford: Blackwell, 318–66.

McGurk, H. and J. MacDonald (1976) 'Hearing lips and seeing voices,' *Nature* 264: 746–8.

Marantz, A. (1982) 'Re reduplication,' *Linguistic Inquiry* 13: 435–82.

Nespor, M. and I. Vogel (1986) *Prosodic Phonology*, Dordrecht: Foris.

Ohala, J. J. (1989) 'Sound change is drawn from a pool of synchronic variation,' in L. E. Breivik and E. H. Jahr (eds), *Language Change: Contributions to the Study of its Causes*, Berlin: Mouton de Gruyter, 173–98.

Pierrehumbert, J. and M. Beckman (1989) *Japanese Tone Structure* (Linguistic Inquiry Monograph, 15), Cambridge, MA: MIT Press.

Postal, P. (1968) *Aspects of Phonological Theory*, New York: Harper & Row.

Prince, A. (1983) 'Relating to the grid,' *Linguistic Inquiry* 14: 19–100.

Prince, A. and P. Smolensky (1993) *Optimality Theory: Constraint Interaction in Generative Grammar*. Ms, Rutgers University and University of Colorado.

Ringen, C. (1988) *Vowel Harmony: Theoretical Implications*, New York: Garland.

Sapir, E. (1933) 'The psychological reality of phonemes,' reprinted in D. Mandelbaum (ed.), *Selected Writings of Edward Sapir in Language, Culture and Personality*, Berkeley, CA: University of California Press.

Saussure, F. de (1916) *Cours de linguistique général*, Paris: Bayot. English translation W. Baskin (1959) *Course in General Linguistics*, New York: Philosophical Library. See also the translation by R. Harris (1983) *F. de Saussure: Course in General Linguistics*, London: Duckworth.

Selkirk, E. (1984) *Phonology and Syntax: The Relation between Sound and Structure*, Cambridge, MA: MIT Press.

Trubetzkoy, N. (1939) *Grundzüge der Phonologie*. Travaux du cercle linguistique de Prague, 7. French translation by J. Cantineau (1949) *Principes de phonologie*, Paris: Klincksieck.

Vihman, M. M. (1996) *Phonological Development*, Oxford: Blackwell.

Wang, W. (1967) 'The phonological features of tone,' *International Journal of American Linguistics* 33: 93–105.

Wells, J. C. (1982) *Accents of English*, vols 1–3, Cambridge: Cambridge University Press.

Yip, M. (1980) *The Tonal Phonology of Chinese*. MIT PhD. Published in New York by Garland in 1990.

Also Available from Edinburgh University Press

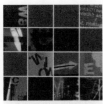

An Introduction to English Phonology
April McMahon

An Introduction to English Phonology introduces undergraduates to the basic tools and concepts necessary for the outline description of English phonological systems and processes.

An Introduction to English Phonology
April McMahon

November 2001
160pp
Pb 978 0 7486 1251 2

By working through the book and the various exercises included, students should come to understand the need for a dedicated system of description and transcription for speech sounds, and for a degree of phonological abstraction. They should learn to carry out elementary, broad phonetic transcription, and be able to establish contrastive vowel and consonant systems for their own varieties and to express simple generalisations reflecting the productive and predictable patterns of English sounds.

Key Features
*   designed for a one-term or one-semester introductory course in English Language
*   suitable for both native and non-native speakers of English
*   emphasis on varieties of modern English around the world
*   an essentially theory-neutral approach, with the concepts central to the practice of phonology clearly explained

April McMahon is Forbes Professor of English Language at the University of Edinburgh.

Edinburgh
University Press

See more Language & Linguistics books at
www.euppublishing.com

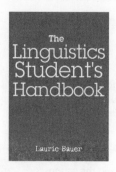

The Linguistics Student's Handbook
Laurie Bauer

The book that tells you all the things you felt you were expected to know about linguistics, but were afraid to ask about.

- What do you know about Burushaski and Miwok?
- What's the difference between paradigmatic and syntagmatic?
- What is E-language?
- What is a language?
- Do parenthetical and non-restrictive mean the same thing?
- How do you write a bibiliographic entry for a work you have not seen?

Every student who has asked these questions needs this book. A compendium of useful things for linguistics students to know, from the IPA chart to the Saussurean dichotomies, this book will be the constant companion of anyone undertaking studies of linguistics. Part reference work, part revision guide, and with tables providing summary information on some 280 languages, the book provides a new learning tool as a supplement to the usual textbooks and glossaries.

Laurie Bauer is Professor of Linguistics at the Victoria University of Wellington.

April 2007
400pp
Pb 978 0 7486 2759 2